ATOMIC GHOST

1. Photograph used with permission from Los Alamos National Laboratory.

ATOMIC GHOST

POETS RESPOND TO THE NUCLEAR AGE

EDITED BY JOHN BRADLEY

Introduction by Terry Tempest Williams

COFFEE HOUSE PRESS :: MINNEAPOLIS :: MCMXCV

Cover photograph number 91 328, and interior photographs on pages 116, 184, 282, and 296 used by permission of Los Alamos National Laboratory. Thanks to Carol Ahlgren for her photographic research. Thanks to Will Powers for supplying us with "Reactor" type for the title on the cover of this book.

The publishers would like to thank the following funders for assistance which helped make this book possible: Dayton Hudson Foundation on behalf of Dayton's and Target Stores; General Mills Foundation; the Honeywell Foundation; the Jerome Foundation; the Lannan Foundation; The McKnight Foundation; The Andrew W. Mellon Foundation; the National Endowment for the Arts, a federal agency; The Beverly J. and John A. Rollwagen Fund of The Minneapolis Foundation; The St. Paul Companies; and Star Tribune/Cowles Media Foundation. This activity is made possible in part by a grant provided by the Minnesota State Arts Board, through an appropriation by the Minnesota State Legislature.

Coffee House Press books are available to the trade through our primary distributor, Consortium Book Sales & Distribution, 1045 Westgate Drive, Saint Paul, MN 55114. Our books are also available through all major library distributors and jobbers, and through most small press distributors, including Bookpeople, Inland, and Small Press Distribution. For personal orders, catalogs or other information, write to:

Coffee House Press
27 North Fourth Street, Suite 400, Minneapolis, MN 55401

Library of Congress CIP Data
Atomic ghost : poets respond to the nuclear age / edited by John Bradley.
       p. cm.
    Includes index.
       ISBN 1-56689-027-6 (pbk. : acid-free)
  1. Atomic bomb victims—Poetry.   2. Antinuclear movement—Poetry.
3. Nuclear warfare and society—Poetry.   4. American poetry—20th century.   I. Bradley, John, 1950- .

PS595.A84A66 1995   94-29816
811' .54080358—dc20   CIP

10 9 8 7 6 5 4 3 2 1

Contents

PART III—LATE SPRING IN THE NUCLEAR AGE

PART IV—GATHERED AT THE RIVER

Preface

"If there are such things as ghosts," says a Japanese woman in Andrew H. Leighton's essay, "That Day at Hiroshima," "why don't they haunt the Americans?"

Judging by the poems in this anthology, and the hundreds of poems submitted for it, they do. They haunt us in many ways. There is the fear for the safety of family and children and our children's children. There is the fear for survival of the planet. There is the fear and anger over the outright lies our own government has issued concerning a range of health and environmental issues relating to nuclear tests and wastes. The poems speak eloquently on all these topics and more, exposing how nuclear fear has settled into the very marrow of our bones.

But there are some who are haunted by the atomic ghosts and don't even know it. This is how this book began. I was sitting in a cavernous office in an old building on the University of Alabama campus in Tuscaloosa. It was a warm spring day in 1984. There was a sophomore or junior talking with another English instructor about a poem he was having the class write about. I couldn't help but overhear, as my desk was a few feet from her chair. It was a simple, honest question. One that startled me, and still does. In response to an image in Robert Lowell's poem "For the Union Dead," the image of a safe that survives the blast, she asked her question: "What is Hiroshima?"

Her question made me realize that there are Americans who have no idea what happened on August 6, 1945. How the world was changed. How we are still dealing with the consequences, and the "ghosts." Her question made me realize I have an obligation as a teacher, a poet, and a human being living in the twentieth century to try to answer her question, to see that future generations will know, and that they in turn will teach their children. How else, I wonder, can we have peace, can we have a future, if we do not remember?

This book, then, is an attempt to answer that young woman's question. May we keep hearing and asking such questions. May we always be haunted by "the ghosts."

I wish to thank all those who lent their support to this project. Special thanks must go to Coffee House Press, for believing in the anthology, to Ed Dougherty and Bill Witherup, each of whom acted as a contributing editor, and to my wife, Jana, for her patience and understanding.

John Bradley

DeKalb, Illinois

Throwing Flowers at Evil

On August 6, 1995, we will commemorate the fiftieth anniversary of Hiroshima, when America dropped the first nuclear bomb on Japan. On that day, the world changed. Suddenly, with an unimaginable horror we witnessed what Galway Kinnell calls "the fundamental project of technology."

Death eyes—130,000 individuals killed instantly with ninety percent of their city obliterated. Three days later, on August 9, 1945, a second bomb was dropped on Nagasaki. More dead. A wave of slow deaths through radiation sickness was to follow.

What on Earth had we done?

John Bradley, in his anthology *Atomic Ghost,* offers us a collective ritual, a ceremony to heal ourselves through poetry, to find hope in the most heinous of affairs—the culture of nuclear war. He brings together the poets who offer us their words of loss and illumination so that we might never forget, so that we might always remember the power we hold to destroy life. "An allegiance to the real," writes Terrence Des Pres, "for some of us, provokes a dream of redemption."

Let us hear their songs.

"This is a prayer that enters a house/ and touches a lantern to light," writes Linda Hogan. "A prayer against heat/ that burns dark roses from shirts into skin . . ."

Adrienne Rich reminds us how we speak of war, "talking of the danger/ as if it were not ourselves/ as if we were testing anything else."

And Richard Wilbur, in his poem "Advice to a Prophet," writes, "Speak of the world's own change. Though we cannot conceive/ of an undreamt thing, we know to our cost/ how the dreamt cloud crumbles . . . how the view alters. We could believe . . ."

I live in Utah. I have seen "that white flash," the white light in the desert that illuminated buttes and mesas. I have heard the lies ("We find no basis for concluding that harm to any individual has resulted from radioactive fallout"—Atomic Energy Commission booklet, 1950s) and I have seen the evidence after watching, one by one, members of my family die from cancer. I, too, am a "downwinder" from the Nevada Nuclear Test Site where atomic bombs were being tested above ground from January 27, 1951 through July 11, 1962. This American tragedy, this story of deceit and betrayal, has broken my heart. It has not, however, broken my spirit.

Susan Griffin, in her poem "Prayer for Continuation," writes, "You must not let terror overtake you."

I remember the last time I committed civil disobedience at the Nevada Test Site. It was Easter Sunday, 1992, six months before the moratorium to stop nuclear testing in the United States was signed by President George Bush. Chief Raymond Yowell, a Shoshone elder, was presiding over the demonstration. He stood before three thousand or more people who were gathered together in the Mojave Desert. He began drumming and chanting, evoking the spirits of his people and the land. We had brought huge baskets and bowls of flower petals, with the belief that we could throw flowers against evil.

Throwing flowers against evil comes from the Yaqui Easter Ceremony. For several weeks during the Easter season, Yaqui people in southern Arizona reënact the passion play, a ritual they adopted from the Jesuits in the fifteenth century.

For several weeks during the Easter season there is a slow, inexorable build-up of evil against the forces of good. On Holy Saturday, the *fariseos,* or Pharisees, are dressed in black cloaks. They are masked and they march to the slow, steady dirge of haunting flute music. They are carrying the weight of evil that is leaning against the village. In long black capes they forcibly make their way through the crowd of onlookers. Their goal is literally to penetrate the church. They have stolen the body of Christ, they have violated every sense of decency within the community. They have marred and destroyed the sacred.

The *fariseos* charge the church at a full run. As they do this they are showered with flower petals thrown against evil by the children and women who comprise a human gauntlet. The final barrier between the *fariseos* and the community's holy altar is a row of young girls—five, six, seven years old—adorned with crisp white dresses. The girls raise boughs of cottonwood and mesquite, wave them over the *fariseos*. The *fariseos* are repelled. They retreat, take off their black capes, and return to the Sanctuario in confession.

A deer—the Deer Dancer—the most peaceful of animals, covered with flower petals, dances in the middle of the *fariseos*. The *fariseos* have been "changed to good" and are "forgiven."

The universe is restored to balance; health and peace have been returned to the village.

This story was told to me by Richard Nelson, an anthropologist who has attended the Yaqui ceremonies. I asked him if it would be all right to carry this story with me to the Test Site. He felt it would be appropriate, saying, "I think these stories exist for all of us as a way of understanding how to behave in the world."

A few days before the demonstration, my nieces Callie and Sara, and I decided we would visit all the florists in town and ask if they had flowers they would like to donate to heal the Test Site. The florists opened their arms to us, and within a few hours the car was completely filled with flowers: roses, dahlias, daisies, tulips, irises, lilies, chrysanthemums, every type of bloom imaginable.

We brought the flowers home, laid them out on a white sheet in the middle of our living room, and started plucking petals. We placed the greenery outside and organized the flowers in big black bowls and baskets.

While we worked, we told stories. We talked about their grandmother, my mother, and their great-grandmother, and what might have caused their deaths. We talked about the Test Site, about the notion of war, the possibilities of peace, and that we could, in fact, throw flowers against evil, that something this delicate and beautiful could make an extraordinary difference. We discussed the power of gesture.

I never thought about how we would get the flowers to the Test Site given that we were flying to Nevada. But once we arrived at the airport and people saw the flowers, rules disappeared.

"Of course you can carry more than two pieces of luggage onto the plane," the flight attendants said. They happily (and a bit subversively) strapped baskets and bowls of flowers into empty seats.

When we arrived in Las Vegas, various passengers volunteered to carry the flowers outside. The beauty was intoxicating.

Finally, at the Test Site, we placed the baskets of flowers around the barbed wire fences and around the platform where Chief Yowell was drumming. The story was retold of the Yaqui passion play and how the community threw flowers at evil. Chief Yowell never wavered but continued drumming and chanting, drumming and chanting. The children from the audience spontaneously rose and walked toward the baskets and bowls of flowers. They took them into their arms and distributed the petals throughout the crowd. Chief Yowell stopped drumming and spoke: "We will now enter the land like water . . ."

En masse, people moved across the Test Site, ducked under the barbed wire fence, crossed the cattle guard, and infiltrated the desert, sprinkling flowers upon the contaminated landscape.

"There is something older than war," writes the poet Lyn Dalebout.

A few weeks ago, Asakura Yuji, Elica Funatsu, and Yasumichi Fukuzawa were visiting the United States from Japan. They are traveling around the world gathering stories for a new vision of peace that they can offer their children on the anniversaries of Hiroshima and Nagasaki.

"We must never forget," Mr. Fukuzawa said as he bowed to the memories and lives of his relatives who died on August 6, 1945.

"We must always remember—" my niece Callie said as she lowered her head toward him.

Atomic Ghost reminds us. It is the poetry of prayer.

This book is in memory of all those who have lost their lives to the Bomb, in its many forms, and for Gaia, sustainer of life and hope.

"Let the fiery armor
drop away from us all"

—Linda Hogan

CREATION

2. Photograph used with permission from Las Vegas News Bureau.

Creation

Trinity Site, New Mexico
5:30 A.M., July 16, 1945

"Let there be light."
And there was *light.*

 The sun was slow in arriving that morning
though it was no longer dark, was light enough,
and having been born with good eyes, we could see.
We stood on the cool cactus sand which was once
an ocean with a patience we rarely practiced.
It was hard to imagine so much water in this place
of permanent thirst. Motionless, we stood
just as we once waited for our sons to struggle
out of our wives. The labor wasn't long,
but the longest ten seconds of our lives. Ten
seconds, that was all—
 And then the man-made flash—
twice as large as the sun—photographed the moment
in fire. Flames burning the sands,
slashing the face of the calm.
 The ball of thunder strangled
the sky. Reached, blasted, bounced on rocks,
became a perfect tower—taller, wider, whiter
than the Aztecs ever dreamed of or desired.
All the gilded temples where we crossed ourselves
and worshipped perished in the smoke. Everything
surpassed in the new incense. Falling.
On our knees. It seemed to reach for us.

We prayed for it to stop, yet urged it on.
The air exploded hot, grew cold, then hot again
invoking Indian winds to rise, to blow,
to break the earth in half.
    Then it was silent.
Motionless, we stood—the air throwing us
back, and we remembered our selves, our past,
the boyhood houses filled with women's singing.
We rose, surveyed the aftermath of our great
experiment. There was not much damage:
rearranged sand, uprooted bushes, a few dead
rabbits. This was, after all, already a desert,
already named *Jornada del Muerto*, plain
of the no-personed God.
    We had seen. And lived.
We blessed ourselves, smelling the victory.
We put on jubilant smiles in the face
of the outcome. But the smiles fell off
unable to withstand the great success.

    The sun was slow in arriving that morning.
Those of us who bore witness saw it rise
in the new sky, motionless, but it no longer
gave enough light. Now, after many years,
our eyes have grown accustomed to the dark.

ALAN NAPIER

Tulum Saw the Coming

You have to believe children of the Olmecs once dreamed too
as they rested thick-lipped stones on
anvils of flattened earth
like planets that promised them eternity for death
But the act of dividing flesh on hard objects
may resist the give and take of reason
The nucleus of faith always splits   Copan whose stone arms
reach out seeking animal obedience
The stepped pyramids of Tikal abandoned to games
of multi-colored birds
and panthers flashing in dark corridors   Uxmal where
hallucinogenic devotion closed in the self-mutilation of time
And Chichen Itza where even now
Quetzalcoatl's victims rustle in stiff palms broadening to sky
The Mayas had a stone that killed   They fed it
till it screamed and when it ate them they disappeared
But we too are human   We too feed a sacred stone
and it breeds its own food
It eats itself and breeds itself to feed us and eat us
You see how the components
disparate and unnatural to life upset the rhythm of the ear and
heartbeat?   And how the heart can be used
to paint the art of gods?
The computer in the stones told them when to seed
when to fall before storms   even when death should be served
But the eagle and the bear
had disgorged their stomachs and the hearts that were left were
all rotten clean through
No treasure on earth was worth another life

But extinction is to blood what fire is to creation
Tulum saw the coming
watched the approaching ships   and saw the coming of the gods

S.L. WISENBERG

May 28, 1945

Unable to get an appointment with President Truman, Leo Szilard
and two other atomic scientists meet in Spartanburg, SC, with
James F. Byrnes, the soon-to-be Secretary of State, to warn him
that the U.S. bombing of Japan would spark a world-wide nuclear
arms race.

A black car
meets us at the train.
For Dr. Lizard. I have to laugh
but I fear
an omen.
The Negro porter says, No bags, suhs?
and I barely
understand
this thickness of tongue. The city is a garden. America
is a garden. Dirt roads, white
Greek columns, moss. Roses
shaded like the sunset, colors
no one speaks of
in New York or Chicago. Thick white waxy flowers
on trees
with a name like a song.
It is as they said. It is as
Gone with the Wind. Soldiers. Girls
in hats and white dresses, ribbons
the colors of tulips.

It has been six years
since I sent warnings to Paris.

I said, We must have it first.
And now I am trying to stay
the official hand.
I am a MittelEuropean
come to the South, a loser's terrain.
The same sky
I knew in Budapest.

Along the Danube
we gathered ferns
and pressed them
in a book. In Berlin
I studied Maxwell's Demon:
You can break the second law
of thermodynamics
if you guess
correctly. I guessed correctly. I removed
my money
to Switzerland.
I watched an old man bury his silver;
children dug it up,
hungry for potatoes.

The Southern gentleman
shows us the rifles at his hearth
while the grandchildren
of slaves
carry in great bowls of fruit.
The house is cool, the bourbon's cold
and Byrnes says, Don't worry, my friends. The Army tells me
no other country
can make a bomb.

He is a fool. In time,
everyone will crack open the safe.

Pandora becomes
Cassandra.
By the time he begins to listen
the world
will be changed.

Do you know my dreams
Mr. Byrnes? We have slept 20 nights
since the surrender of Europe. Now we talk
of the greater evil
and our tongues become thickened
on sweet gold liquor.
You pat our hands. We are envoys
from a place you do not believe in. But I have seen,
Mr. Byrnes,
flashes
made by invisible objects. I have heard
the silent conversion
of stone into fire.

You cannot comprehend
this ant
that can devour the elephant. Your mind cannot see
past these acres—bloodied, overgrown fields
bounded by white pillars.
And I, a man with no country, cannot move a man
rooted by ghosts
that refuse to divide
into finer universal particles.

KENT JOHNSON

High Altitude Photo of Hiroshima (Circa 1944)

I dedicate this poem to the great artist, Piet Mondrian

March 7, 1957

There must be a schoolgirl deep inside there, stuttering,
almost weeping to remember the main cities
of our ally, Germany.

There must be a monk, self-absorbed, slowly dragging
his rake through sand, around a moss-covered stone.

A man, inside his home, has thrown a little boy into the air:
The child is there, falling, his mouth open with joy.

And I . . . where am I? For being here is confusing,
makes my position less clear. Somewhere in the upper left,
I suppose, hurrying ambitiously to get somewhere . . .

I shut my eyes, try to recall those days . . .

Outside of me the photograph is beautiful and clear:
A long, single pulse of geometry under dreams.
Pure hieroglyph into which I also will vanish.

from *The Daybook of Ogiwara Miyamori*

KIMIKO HAHN

The Bath: August 6, 1945

Bathing the summer night
off my arms and breasts
I heard a plane
overhead *I heard*
the door rattle
froze
then relaxed in the cool water
one more moment
one private moment
before waking the children
and mother-in-law,
before the heat
before the midday heat
drenched my spirits again.
I had wanted
to also relax
in thoughts of my husband—
how we were children
when he was drafted
imprisoned—but didn't dare
and rose from the tub,
dried off lightly
and slipped on cotton work pants.
Caution drew me to the window
and there an enormous blossom of fire
a hand changed my life
and made the world shiver—
a light that tore flesh
so it slipped off limbs,
swelled so

no one could recognize
a mother or child
a hand that tore the door open
pushed me on the floor
ripped me up—
I will never have children again
so even today
my hair has not grown back
my teeth still shards
and one eye blind
and it would be easy,
satisfying somehow
to write it off as history
those men are there
each time I close
my one good eye
each time or lay blame
on men or militarists
the children cry out
in my sleep
where they still live
for the sake of a night's rest.
But it isn't air raids
simply
that we survive
but *gold worth its weight*
in blood the coal,
oil, uranium we mine
and drill
yet cannot call our own.
And it would be gratifying
to be called a survivor
I am a survivor
since I live if I didn't wonder
about survival today—

at 55, widowed at 18—
if I didn't feel
the same oppressive August heat
auto parts in South Africa,
Mexico, Alabama,
and shiver not from memory
or terror
but anger that this wounded body
must stand *take a stand*
and cry out
as only a newborn baby can cry—
I live, I will live
I will to live
in spite of history
to make history
in my vision of peace—
that morning in the bath
so calm
so much my right
though I cannot return to that moment
I bring these words to you
hoping to hold you
to hold you
and to take hold.

MARC KAMINSKY

Questions*

If I shriek
who will hear me
if I don't
break the silence in which diatribes
pile up, who will
hear me
if I speak normal
words in the normal
order

who will hear me

if I make poems
of what I saw and heard on the road
from Hiroshima

will I disturb
the dead

will I
be a merchant of our disaster

if I fail
to work all the horror
into a play
of voices in which the living and the dead
live again

who will forgive me

*Written as Nakajima Hiroshi, a fictional witness.

TŌGE SANKICHI

At the Makeshift Aid Station

You girls—
weeping even though there is no place for tears to come from;
crying out even though you have no lips to shape the words;
reaching out even though there is no skin on your fingers
  to grasp with—
you girls.

Oozing blood and greasy sweat and lymph, your limbs twitch;
puffed to slits, your eyes glitter whitely;
only the elastic bands of your panties hold in your swollen bellies;
though your private parts are exposed, you are
  wholly beyond shame:
to think
that a little while ago
you all were pretty schoolgirls!

Emerging from the flames that flickered gloomily
in burned-out Hiroshima
no longer yourselves,
you rushed out, crawled out one after the other,
struggled along to this grassy spot,
in agony laid your heads, bald but for a few wisps of hair,
  on the ground.

Why must you suffer like this?
Why must you suffer like this?
For what reason?
For what reason?
You girls
don't know

how desperate your condition,
how far transformed from the human.

You are simply thinking,
thinking
of those who until this morning
        were your fathers, mothers, brothers, sisters
(would any of them know you now?)
and of the homes in which you slept, woke, ate
(in that instant the hedgeroses were torn off; who knows
        what has become of their ashes?)

thinking, thinking—
as you lie there among friends who one after the other
        stop moving—
thinking
of when you were girls,
human beings.

                    translated from the Japanese by Richard H. Minear

PHILIP LEVINE

The Horse

for Ichiro Kawamoto, humanitarian,
electrician, & survivor of Hiroshima

They spoke of the horse alive
without skin, naked, hairless,
without eyes and ears, searching
for the stableboy's caress.
Shoot it, someone said, but they
let him go on colliding with
tattered walls, butting his long
skull to pulp, finding no path
where iron fences corkscrewed in
the street and bicycles turned
like question marks.
                    Some fled and
some sat down. The river burned
all that day and into the
night, the stones sighed a moment
and were still, and the shadow
of a man's hand entered
a leaf.
            The white horse never
returned, and later they found
the stable boy, his back crushed
by a hoof, his mouth opened
around a cry that no one heard.

They spoke of the horse again
and again; their mouths opened
like the gills of a fish caught
above water.

Mountain flowers
burst from the red clay walls, and
they said a new life was here.
Raw grass sprouted from the cobbles
like hair from a deafened ear.
The horse would never return.

There had been no horse. I could
tell from the way they walked
testing the ground for some cold
that the rage had gone out of
their bones in one mad dance.

JAMES TATE

Land of Little Sticks, 1945

Where the wife is scouring the frying pan
and the husband is leaning up against the barn.
Where the boychild is pumping water into a bucket
and the girl is chasing a spotted dog.

And the sky churns on the horizon.
A town by the name of Pleasantville has disappeared.
And now the horses begin to shift and whinny,
and the chickens roost, keep looking this way and that.
At this moment something is not quite right.

The boy trundles through the kitchen, spilling water.
His mother removes several pies from the oven, shouts at him.
The girlchild sits down by the fence to stare at the horses.
And the man is just as he was, eyes closed, forehead
against his forearm, leaning up against the barn.

KENT JOHNSON

Trilobytes

I dedicate this poem to the potter, Sakutaro Ishihara, (1897–1947)

December 15, 1947

Only last month I was drunk with him
in Koi, at the Soto Bar. He had come
from his treatment and seemed overly excited.

Suddenly from his burlap-bag, he raised
a concave stone, and placed it, gently,
in the space between us.

And what have we here?, I said, with a great curiosity.

The fossils of trilobytes!, he whispered, leaning
forward, as if sharing a sexual secret.

(The waiter appeared over us, clutching a vase
of sake, his long geisha-nails like contrails
against the black lacquer . . .)

Where on earth did you come upon this?, I inquired.

Why at the Central Museum . . .
A fossil collection donated by the Americans . . .
A challenge to get past the guards!

We both laughed deeply then, and for a moment
I could see, beneath the scarred flesh,
the beautiful face of his youth . . .

I gazed at him, gazing at the fossil:
The clumps of hair on his skull; the hands
curled into claws. Was he thinking
of his pottery, all of it, scattered into atoms?

This morning, I cradled the stone
through the ruins, past the shadows of bodies
and bowing to his memory,
placed it,
soundlessly,
at the epicenter.

from *The Daybook of Ogiwara Miyamori*

The Shadow

Cheap movie theaters, saloons, fly-by-night markets,
burned, rebuilt, standing, crumbling, spreading like the itch—
the new Hiroshima,
head shiny with hair oil,
barefaced in its resurgence;
already visible all over the place,
in growing numbers, billboards in English;
one of these: "Historic A-Bomb Site."

Enclosed by a painted fence
on a corner of the bank steps,
stained onto the grain of the dark red stone:
a quiet pattern.

That morning
a flash tens of thousands of degrees hot
burned it all of a sudden onto the thick slab of granite:
someone's trunk.

Burned onto the step, cracked and watery red,
the mark of the blood that flowed as intestines melted to mush:
a shadow.

Ah! If you are from Hiroshima
and on that morning,
amid indescribable flash and heat and smoke,
were buffeted in the whirlpool of the glare of the flames, the
        shadow of the cloud,
crawled about dragging skin that was peeling off,
so transformed that even your wife and children

would not have known you,
this shadow
is etched in tragic memory
and will never fade.

Right beside the street where the people of the city come and go,
well-meaning but utterly indifferent,
assaulted by the sun, attacked by the rain, covered over by dust,
growing fainter year by year: this shadow.

The bank with the "Historic Site" sign at the foot of the steps
dumped out into the street pieces of stone and glass, burned
        gritty,
completed a major reconstruction,
and set the whole enormous building sparkling in the evening
        sun.
In the vacant lot diagonally across,
drawing a crowd: a quack in the garb of a mountain ascetic.

Indifferent, the authorities say: "If we don't protect it with glass
        or something,
it will fade away," but do nothing.
Today, too,
foreign sailors amble up in their white leggings,
come to a stop with a click of their heels,
and, each having taken a snapshot, go off;
the shoeshine boy who followed them here
peers over the fence, wonders why all the fuss,
and goes on his way.

                    translated from the Japanese by Richard H. Minear

JOHN ENGELS

The Fish Dream

In Bikini when as sudden
as the mirror of a wing
the light came, the wind changed,

and hot dust mucked
our crannies up,
we locked ourselves below,

turned off the air, and stack gas
filled the passageways, topside
the flight deck bloomed

with a thousand fountains,
and below decks six times a day
we took saltwater showers

and held our breaths. Later
we'd lie like stains
in our sodden bunks,

and it made for dreams—umber-
scaled and yellow-spotted fish
with six-inch needle teeth

crept out on fleshy fins across
the blazing decks and gorged our heads
while we stared on, afraid to wake.

JOHN BRADLEY

Sailors Shielding Their Eyes During Atomic Bomb Test, Bikini, 1947

Light,
unbearable
light

Is what moves
your head
into the crook of your arm,
slides your other arm
across your chest
in a tight
half-embrace.

Face buried, eyes
shut, you can see
someone in white,
years from now,
with a knife too sharp
to feel, slicing
along your testicles.

Will the seed
you carry be able to spawn
a child
impervious to the might
you witnessed, back
at Bikini?

Or did the flash
bloom a cancer

3. Photograph by Fritz Goro. Permission granted by Life magazine © Time Warner Inc.

there in the darkness
of your scrotum?

You strain to hear
the words of the doctor—
It's a blessing,
he tells you. Or does he say—
It's for the best?

You press your head
deeper
into the crook of your arm.

TŌGE SANKICHI

August 6, 1950

They come running;
they come running.
From that side, from this,
hands on holstered pistols,
the police come on the run.

August 6, 1950:
the Peace Ceremony has been banned;
on street corners at night, on bridge approaches at dawn,
the police standing guard are restive.
Today, at the very center of Hiroshima—
the Hatchobori intersection,
in the shadow of the F. Department Store—

the stream of city folk who have come to place flowers
at memorials, at ruins,
suddenly becomes a whirlpool;
chin-straps taut with sweat
plunge into the crowd;
split by the black battle-line,
reeling,
the crowd as one looks up at the department store—
from fifth-floor windows, sixth-floor windows,
fluttering,
fluttering,
against the backdrop of summer clouds,
now in shadow, now in sunlight,
countless handbills dance
and scatter slowly
over upturned faces,
into outstretched hands,

into the depths of empty hearts.
People pick them up off the ground;
arms swing and knock them out of the air;
hands grab them in midair;
eyes read them:
workers, merchants, students, girls,
old people and children from outlying villages—
a throng of residents representing all Hiroshima
for whom August 6 is the anniversary of a death—and the police:
pushing, shoving. Angry cries.
The urgent appeal
of the peace handbills they reach for,
the antiwar handbills they will not be denied.
Streetcars stop;
traffic lights topple;
jeeps roll up;
fire sirens scream;
riot trucks drive up—two trucks, three;
an expensive foreign car forces its way
through the ranks of police in plain clothes;
the entrance to the department store becomes a grim checkpoint.

Still handbills fall,
gently, gently.
Handbills catch on the canopy; hands appear, holding a broom,
sweep every last one off;
they dance their way down
one by one, like living things,
like voiceless shouts,
lightly, lightly.

The Peace Ceremony—the releasing of doves, the ringing of bells,
the mayor's peace message carried off on the breeze—
is stamped out like a child's sparkler;
all gatherings are banned:

speeches,
concerts,
the UNESCO meeting;
Hiroshima is under occupation by armed police and police in
        mufti.

The smoke of rocket launchers
rises from newsreel screens;
from back streets resound the shouts
of those, children too, who signed petitions against the bomb.
In the sky over Hiroshima on August 6, 1950,
spreading light above anxious residents,
casting shadows on silent graveyards,
toward you who love peace,
toward me who wants peace,
drawing the police on the double,
handbills fall,
handbills fall.

        translated from the Japanese by Richard H. Minear

Uranium

Red-faced and sweating in autumn
heat, Grandpa and his khaki friend
from town unloaded picks and hammers
off the truck, and took out a case
with dials that seemed a radio
or recording machine with spiral
cord and microphone and needles.
All afternoon they circled fields
and pasture gullies, climbed the ledge
above the road, knocked on spoil of
the old zircon digs, chipped at
the cliff face, and shoveled mud from
the branch bed. Each time they found
a specimen they put the mike
to its gritty form and listened,
and checked the needles' sway. The crops
were in and Grandpa looked for a new
harvest in the soil. I watched them
lug the equipment and armloads
of rocks like apples to the truck,
and knew the Russians might blow us
up any day, they said, and what
they looked for bombs were made of. At
the barn they let me listen to
the counter's faint static. And while
the old men talked of wealth and sure
Armageddon and the Bible's
plans for our annihilation
I heard the white chatter of rock,
a noise that seemed to go back in

time inside the bright machine, and
inside the hammered flakes in hand,
to the crackle of creation's
distant fires still whispering in us.

ADRIENNE RICH

For Ethel Rosenberg

convicted, with her husband,
of "conspiracy to commit
espionage"; killed in the
electric chair June 19, 1953

I.

Europe 1953:
throughout my random sleepwalk
the words

scratched on walls, on pavements
painted over railway arches
Liberez les Rosenberg!

Escaping from home I found
home everywhere:
the Jewish question, Communism

marriage itself
a question of loyalty
or punishment

my Jewish father writing me
letters of seventeen pages
finely inscribed harangues

questions of loyalty
and punishment
One week before my wedding

that couple gets the chair
the volts grapple her, don't
kill her fast enough

Liberez les Rosenberg!
I hadn't realized
our family arguments were so important

my narrow understanding
of crime   of punishment
no language for this torment

mystery of that marriage
always both faces
on every front page in the world

Something so shocking   so
unfathomable
it must be pushed aside

II.

She sank however into my soul   A weight of sadness
I hardly can register how deep
her memory has sunk   that wife and mother

like so many
who seemed to get nothing out of any of it
except her children

that daughter   of a family
like so many
needing its female monster

she, actually wishing to be   *an artist*
wanting out of poverty
possibly also really wanting
                              revolution

that woman   strapped in the chair
no fear and no regrets
charged by posterity

not with selling secrets to the Communists
but with wanting   *to distinguish*
herself being a bad daughter   a bad mother

And I   walking to my wedding
by the same token a bad daughter   a bad sister
my forces focused

on that hardly revolutionary effort
Her life and death   the possible
ranges of disloyalty

so painful so unfathomable
they must be pushed aside
ignored for years

III.

Her mother testifies against her
Her brother testifies against her
After her death

she becomes a natural prey for pornographers
her death itself a scene
her body *sizzling   half-strapped   whipped like a sail*

She becomes the extremest victim
described nonetheless as *rigid of will*
what are her politics by then   no one knows

Her figure sinks into my soul
a drowned statue
sealed in lead

For years it has lain there   unabsorbed
first as part of that dead couple
on the front pages of the world   the week

I gave myself in marriage
then slowly severing   drifting apart
a separate death   a life unto itself

no longer *the Rosenbergs*
no longer the chosen scapegoat
the family monster

till I hear how she sang
a prostitute to sleep
in the Women's House of Detention

Ethel Greenglass Rosenberg   would you
have marched to take back the night
collected signatures

for battered women who kill
What would you have to tell us
would you have burst the net

IV.

Why do I even want to call her up
to console my pain   (she feels no pain at all)
why do I wish to put such questions

to ease myself   (she feels no pain at all
she   finally burned to death   like so many)
why all this exercise of hindsight?

since   if I imagine her at all
I have to imagine first
the pain inflicted on her   by women

her mother testifies against her
her sister-in-law testifies against her
and how she sees it

not the impersonal forces
not the historical reasons
why they might have hated her strength

If I have held her at arm's length till now
if I have still believed it was
my loyalty, my punishment at stake

if I dare imagine her surviving
I must be fair to what she must have lived through
I must allow her to be at last

political in her ways   not in mine
her urgencies perhaps   impervious to mine
defining revolution as she defines it

or, bored to the marrow of her bones
with "politics"
bored with the vast boredom of long pain

small; tiny in fact; in her late sixties
liking her room   her private life
living alone perhaps

no one you could interview
maybe filling a notebook herself
with secrets she has never sold

1980

But Bird

Some things you should forget,
But Bird was something to believe in.
Autumn 1954, twenty, drafted,
Stationed near New York, en route
To the atomic tests in Nevada.
I taught myself to take
A train to Pennsylvania Station,
Walk up Seventh to 52d Street,
Looking for music and legends.
One night I found the one
I wanted. Bird.

Five months later no one was brave
When the numbers ran out.
All equal—privates, sergeants,
Lieutenants, majors, colonels—
All down on our knees in the slits
As the voice counted backward
In the darkness turning to light.

But "Charlie Parker" it said
On the Birdland marquee,
And I dug for the cover charge,
Sat down in the cheap seats.
He slumped in from the kitchen,
Powder blue serge and suedes.
No jive Bird, he blew crisp and clean,
Bringing each face in the crowd
Gleaming to the bell of his horn.
No fluffing, no wavering,

But soaring like on my old
Verve waxes back in Ohio,
He smiled, nodding to applause.

Months later, down in the sand,
The bones in our fingers were
Suddenly x-rayed by the flash.
We moaned together in light
That entered everything,
Tried to become the earth itself
As the shock rolled toward us.

But Bird. I sat through three sets,
Missed the last train out,
Had to bunk in a roach pad,
Sleep in my uniform, almost AWOL.
But Bird was giving it all away,
One of his last great gifts,
And I was there with my
Rosy cheeks and swan neck,
Looking for something to believe in.

When the trench caved in it felt
Like death, but we clawed out,
Walked beneath the roiling, brutal cloud
To see the flattened houses,
Sheep and pigs blasted,
Ravens and rabbits blind,
Scrabbling in the grit and yucca.

But Bird. Remember Bird,
Though of course he was gone.
Five months later, dead,
While I was down on my knees,
Wretched with fear in
The cinders of the desert.

DAVID MURA

The "Hibakusha's" Letter (1955)

Survivors of the atomic bomb were called hibakusha. This name became associated with keloids, a whitish-yellow scar tissue, and later, with defects, disease, and disgrace.

The fields, Teruko-san, are threshed. A good
Harvest. All week I've seen farmers with torches
Bend to earth, releasing fires. The winds
Sweep ash across the roads, dirty my laundry

Hung on the fence. Prayer drums, gongs, clap
In the streets, and now the village celebrates.
Last night Matsuo told me how he emptied
On a clump of rags beside the inn. Suddenly

The clump jumped up, groggy, wet, cursing.
Matsuo finished, bowed, offered him a drink.
This morning I shuffled out back to gossip
With my neighbor, an eighty-year-old woman

Who prances like a mouse about her garden.
While she jabbered Matsuo cut her firewood;
Sweat poured from the scars he no longer marks.
Later I opened my shrine to its brass Buddha,

And fruit flies scattered from the bowl of plums
I'd forgotten to change. Pulled from the rubble,
Burnt at the edges, my fiancé's picture
Crumbled in my fingers. I lit him incense.

Matsuo says we can't drag each corpse behind us
Like a shadow. The eye blinks, a world's gone,
And the slow shudder at our shoulders says
We won't be back. This year I've changed my diet:

I eat only rice, *utskemono, tofu.*
Sashimi sickens me, passion for raw meat.
Sister, remember how Mother strangled chickens?
She twirled them in the air by their necks.

Like a boy with a slingshot. I'd watch in horror
Their bodies twitch, hung from her fist, and cry
That Buddha kept their karma in my stomach.
Like them we had no warning. Flames filled kimonos

With limbs of ash, and I wandered past
Smoldering trolleys away from the city.
Of course you're right. We can't even play beauty
Or the taste of steel quickens our mouths.

I can't conceive, and though Matsuo says
It doesn't matter, my empty belly haunts me:
Why call myself a woman, him a man,
If on our island only ghosts can gather?

And yet, I can't deny it. There are times,
Teruko, I am happy . . .
You say *hibakusha* should band together. Here
Fewer eyes shower us in shame. I wandered

Too far: My death flashed without, not within.
I can't come back. To beg the world's forgiveness
Gains so little, and monuments mean nothing.
I can't choose your way or even Matsuo's:

"Drink, Yoshiki, *sake's* the one surgeon
Doesn't cost or cut." This evening, past fields black
And steaming, the pitch of night soil, I'll wander
Up foothills to the first volcanic springs.

After a wind from hell, the smell of burning
Now seems sweeter than flowers . . .

Early Morning Test Light
over Nevada, 1955

Your mother slept through it all,
her face turned away
like the dark side of the earth.

We'd heard
between *rancheras* on the radio
that the ladles
and the two bears
that lie among the stars
above Nevada
would fade at 3:15 as though seared
by a false sun.

The stove exhaled all night
a trinity of blue rings. You entered
your fourth month
of floating in the tropical,
star-crossed water
your mother carried under her heart
that opens and closes
like a butterfly.

When the sky flared,
our room lit up. Cobwebs
sparkled on the walls, and a spider
absorbed the light
like a chameleon and began
to inch toward the outer rings
as if a fly trembled.

Roosters crowed. The dog
scratched at the door. I went outside
hearing the hens and thought *weasel*
and found broken eggs, the chicks
spongy, their eyes
stunned and shrouded
by thin veils of skin.

"Don't open your eyes,"
I whispered to you when darkness
returned. I thought of your bones
still a white gel, I remembered the story
of blood smeared on doorways,
and I placed my hand on the balloon
you rode in—that would slowly sink
to your birth. I said
the Old German name your mother already picked
for you, *Robert*. It means *bright fame*.

The Planet Krypton

Outside the window the McGill smelter
sent a red dust down on the smoking yards of copper,
on the railroad tracks' frayed ends disappearing
into the congestion of the afternoon. Ely lay dull

and scuffed: a miner's boot toe worn away and dim,
while my mother knelt before the Philco to coax
the detonation from the static. From the Las Vegas
Tonapah Artillery and Gunnery Range the sound

of the atom bomb came biting like a swarm
of bees. We sat in the hot Nevada dark, delighted,
when the switch was tripped and the bomb hoisted
up its silky, hooded, glittering, uncoiled length;

it hissed and spit, it sizzled like a poker in a toddy.
The bomb was no mind and all body; it sent a fire
of static down the spine. In the dark it glowed like the coils
of an electric stove. It stripped every leaf from every

branch until a willow by a creek was a bouquet
of switches resinous, naked, flexible, and fine.
Bathed in the light of KDWN, Las Vegas,
my crouched mother looked radioactive, swampy,

glaucous, like something from the Planet Krypton.
In the suave, brilliant wattage of the bomb, we were
not poor. In the atom's fizz and pop we heard possibility
uncorked. Taffeta wraps whispered on davenports.

A new planet bloomed above us; in its light
the stumps of cut pine gleamed like dinner plates.
The world was beginning all over again, fresh and hot;
we could have anything we wanted.

Bomb

Budger of history   Brake of time   You   Bomb
Toy of universe   Grandest of all snatched-sky   I cannot hate you
Do I hate the mischievous thunderbolt   the jawbone of an ass
The bumpy club of One Million B.C.   the mace   the flail   the axe
Catapult Da Vinci   tomahawk Cochise   flintlock Kidd   dagger Rathbone
Ah and the sad desperate gun of Verlaine   Pushkin   Dillinger   Bogart
And hath not St. Michael a burning sword   St. George a lance   Christ a whip   David a sling
Bomb   you are as cruel as man makes you   and you're no crueller than cancer
All man hates you   they'd rather die by car-crash   lightning   drowning
Falling off a roof   electric-chair   heart-attack   old age   old age   O Bomb
They'd rather die by anything but you   Death's finger is free-lance
Not up to man whether you boom or not   Death has long since distributed its
categorical blue   I sing thee Bomb   Death's extravagance   Death's jubilee
Gem of Death's supremest blue   The flyer will crash   his death will differ
with the climber who'll fall   To die by cobra is not to die by bad pork
Some die by swamp   some by sea   and some by the bushy-haired man in the night
O there are deaths like witches of Arc   Scary deaths like Boris Karloff
No-feeling deaths like birth-death   sadless deaths like old pain Bowery
Abandoned deaths   like Capital Punishment   stately deaths like senators
And unthinkable deaths like Harpo Marx   girls on Vogue covers   my own
I do not know just how horrible Bombdeath is   I can only imagine
Yet no other death I know has so laughable a preview   I scope
a city   New York City   streaming   starkeyed   subway shelter
Scores and scores   A fumble of humanity   High heels bend
Hats whelming away   Youth forgetting their combs
Ladies not knowing what to do   with their shopping bags
Unperturbed gum machines   Yet dangerous 3d rail
Ritz Brothers   from the Bronx   caught in the A Train
The smiling Schenley poster will always smile
Impish Death   Satyr Bomb   Bombdeath

Turtles exploding over Istanbul
The jaguar's flying foot
soon to sink in arctic snow
Penguins plunged against the Sphinx
The top of the Empire State
arrowed in a broccoli field in Sicily
Eiffel shaped like a C in Magnolia Gardens
St. Sophia peeling over Sudan
O athletic Death   Sportive Bomb
The temples of ancient times
their grand ruin ceased
Electrons   Protons   Neutrons
gathering Hesperean hair
walking the dolorous golf of Arcady
joining marble helmsmen
entering the final amphitheater
with a hymnody feeling of all Troys
heralding cypressean torches
racing plumes and banners
and yet knowing Homer with a step of grace
Lo the visiting team of Present
the home team of Past
Lyre and tuba together joined
Hark the hotdog soda olive grape
gala galaxy robed and uniformed
commissary   O the happy stands
Ethereal root and cheer and boo
The billioned all-time attendance
The Zeusian pandemonium
Hermes racing Owens
the Spitball of Buddha
Christ striking out
Luther stealing third
Planetarium Death   Hosannah Bomb
Gush the final rose   O Spring Bomb

Come with thy gown of dynamite green
unmenace Nature's inviolate eye
Before you the wimpled Past
behind you the hallooing Future   O Bomb
Bound in the grassy clarion air
like the fox of the tally-ho
thy field the universe thy hedge the geo
Leap Bomb   bound Bomb   frolic zig and zag
The stars a swarm of bees in thy binging bag
Stick angels on your jubilee feet
wheels of rainlight on your bunky seat
You are due and behold you are due
and the heavens are with you
hosannah incalescent glorious liaison
BOMB O havoc antiphony molten cleft BOOM
Bomb mark infinity a sudden furnace
spread thy multitudinous encompassed Sweep
set forth awful agenda
Carrion stars   charnel planets   carcass elements
Corpse the universe   tee-hee finger-in-the-mouth hop
over its long long dead Nor
From thy nimbled matted spastic eye
exhaust deluges of celestial ghouls
From thy appellational womb
spew birth-gusts of great worms
Rip open your belly Bomb
inform your belly to outflock vulturic salutations
Battle forth your spangled hyena finger stumps
along the brink of Paradise
O Bomb   O final Pied Piper
both sun and firefly behind your shock waltz
God abandoned mock-nude
beneath His thin false-tale'd apocalypse
He cannot hear thy flute's
happy-the-day profanations

He is spilled deaf into the Silencer's warty ear
His Kingdom an eternity of crude wax
Clogged clarions untrumpet Him
Sealed angels unsing Him
A thunderless God   A dead God
O Bomb   thy BOOM His tomb
That I lean forward on a desk of science
an astrologer dabbling in dragon prose
half-smart about wars   bombs   especially bombs
That I am unable to hate what is necessary to love
That I can't exist in a world that consents
a child in a park   a man dying in an electric-chair
That I am able to laugh at all things
all that I know and do not know   thus to conceal my pain
That I say I am a poet and therefore love all man
knowing my words to be the acquainted prophecy of all men
and my unwords no less an acquaintanceship
That I am manifold
a man pursuing the big lies of gold
or a poet roaming in bright ashes
or that which I imagine myself to be
a shark-toothed sleep   a man-eater of dreams
I need not then be all-smart about bombs
Happily so   for if I felt bombs were caterpillars
I'd doubt not they'd become butterflies
There is a hell for bombs
They're there   I see them there
They sit in bits and sing songs
mostly German songs
and two very long American songs
and they wish there were more songs
especially Russian and Chinese songs
and some more very long American songs
Poor little Bomb that'll never be
an Eskimo song   I love thee

I want to put a lollipop
in thy furcal mouth
A wig of Goldilocks on thy baldy bean
and have you skip with me Hansel and Gretel
along the Hollywoodian screen
O Bomb in which all lovely things
moral and physical anxiously participate
O fairyflake plucked from the
grandest universe tree
O piece of heaven which gives
both mountain and anthill a sun
I am standing before your fantastic lily door
I bring you Midgardian roses   Arcadian musk
Reputed cosmetics from the girls of heaven
Welcome me   fear not thy opened door
nor thy cold ghost's grey memory
nor the pimps of indefinite weather
their cruel terrestrial thaw
Oppenheimer is seated
in the dark pocket of Light
Fermi is dry in Death's Mozambique
Einstein his mythmouth
a barnacled wreath on the moon-squid's head
Let me in   Bomb   rise from that pregnant-rat corner
fear not the raised-broom nations of the world
O Bomb I love you
I want to kiss your clank   eat your boom
You are a paean   an acme of scream
a lyric hat of Mister Thunder
O resound thy tanky knees
BOOM   BOOM   BOOM   BOOM   BOOM
BOOM ye skies and BOOM ye suns
BOOM BOOM ye moons   ye stars BOOM
nights ye BOOM   ye days ye BOOM
BOOM BOOM ye winds   ye clouds ye rains

go BANG ye lakes   ye oceans BING
Barracuda BOOM and cougar BOOM
Ubangi BANG   orangoutang
BING BANG BONG BOOM   bee bear baboon
ye BANG ye BONG ye BING
the tail the fin the wing
Yes   Yes   into our midst a bomb will fall
Flowers will leap in joy their roots aching
Fields will kneel proud beneath the hallelujahs of the wind
Pinkbombs will blossom   Elkbombs will perk their ears
Ah many a bomb that day will awe the bird a gentle look
Yet   not enough to say a bomb will fall
or even contend celestial fire goes out
Know that the earth will madonna the Bomb
that in the hearts of men to come more bombs will be born
magisterial bombs wrapped in ermine   all beautiful
and they'll sit plunk on earth's grumpy empires
fierce with moustaches of gold

ADRIAN C. LOUIS

Nevada Red Blues

Where live fire began to inhabit you.
—Pablo Neruda

We live under
slot machine
stars
that jackpot
into the black
velvet
backdrop
and
mirror the greed
of the creatures who soiled our land.

Numa,
it was
not
enough
for
Taibo
to make
our sacred land
a living
though
pustulous
whore.

4. Photograph used with permission from Las Vegas News Bureau.

He
had
to drop
hydrogen bombs
where
thousands
of years
of our blood
spirits lie.

Note: *Numa* is Paiute Indian for "the people" and *Taibo* for "white man."

DENISE LEVERTOV

Watching "Dark Circle"

"This *is* hell, nor am I out of it"
      —Marlowe, *Dr. Faustus*

Men are willing to observe
the writhing, the bubbling flesh and
swift but protracted charring of bone
while the subject pigs, placed in cages designed for this,
don't pass out but continue to scream as they turn to cinder.
The Pentagon wants to know
something a child could tell it:
it hurts to burn, and even a match
can make you scream, pigs or people,
even the smallest common flame can kill you.
This plutonic calefaction is redundant.

Men are willing
to call the roasting of live pigs
a simulation of certain conditions. It is
not a simulation. The pigs (with their high‑rated intelligence,
their uncanny precognition of disaster) are real,
their agony real agony, the smell
is not archetypal breakfast nor ancient feasting
but a foul miasma irremovable from the nostrils,
and the simulation of hell these men
have carefully set up
is hell itself,
           and they in it, dead in their lives,
and what can redeem them? What can redeem them?

Note: *Dark Circle* (1982) is a film produced by Chris Beaver, Judy Irving, and Ruth Landy of the Independent Documentary Group.

ADRIENNE RICH

Trying to Talk with a Man

Out in this desert we are testing bombs,

that's why we came here.

Sometimes I feel an underground river
forcing its way between deformed cliffs
an acute angle of understanding
moving itself like a locus of the sun
into this condemned scenery.

What we've had to give up to get here—
whole LP collections, films we starred in
playing in the neighborhoods, bakery windows
full of dry, chocolate-filled Jewish cookies,
the language of love-letters, of suicide notes,
afternoons on the riverbank
pretending to be children.

Coming out to this desert
we meant to change the face of
driving among dull green succulents
walking at noon in the ghost town
surrounded by a silence

that sounds like the silence of the place
except that it came with us
and is familiar
and everything we were saying until now
was an effort to blot it out—
coming out here we are up against it

Out here I feel more helpless
with you than without you

You mention the danger
and list the equipment
we talk of people caring for each other
in emergencies—laceration, thirst—
but you look at me like an emergency

Your dry heat feels like power
your eyes are stars of a different magnitude
they reflect lights that spell out: EXIT
when you get up and pace the floor

talking of the danger
as if it were not ourselves
as if we were testing anything else.

1971

Advice to a Prophet

When you come, as you soon must, to the streets of our city,
Mad-eyed from stating the obvious,
Not proclaiming our fall but begging us
In God's name to have self-pity,

Spare us all word of the weapons, their force and range,
The long numbers that rocket the mind;
Our slow, unreckoning hearts will be left behind,
Unable to fear what is too strange.

Nor shall you scare us with talk of the death of the race.
How should we dream of this place without us?—
The sun mere fire, the leaves untroubled about us,
A stone look on the stone's face?

Speak of the world's own change. Though we cannot conceive
Of an undreamt thing, we know to our cost
How the dreamt cloud crumbles, the vines are blackened by frost,
How the view alters. We could believe,

If you told us so, that the white-tailed deer will slip
Into perfect shade, grown perfectly shy,
The lark avoid the reaches of our eye,
The jack-pine lose its knuckled grip

On the cold ledge, and every torrent burn
As Xanthus once, its gliding trout
Stunned in a twinkling. What should we be without
The dolphin's arc, the dove's return,

These things in which we have seen ourselves and spoken?
Ask us, prophet, how we shall call
Our natures forth when that live tongue is all
Dispelled, that glass obscured or broken

In which we have said the rose of our love and the clean
Horse of our courage, in which beheld
The singing locust of the soul unshelled,
And all we mean or wish to mean.

Ask us, ask us whether with the worldless rose
Our hearts shall fail us; come demanding
Whether there shall be lofty or long standing
When the bronze annals of the oak-tree close.

The Testimony of J. Robert Oppenheimer

A Fiction

When I attained enlightenment,
I threw off the night like an old skin.
My eyes filled with light
and I fell to the ground.
I lay in Los Alamos,
while at the same time,
I fell
toward Hiroshima,
faster and faster,
till the earth,
till the morning
slipped away beneath me.
Some say when I hit
there was an explosion,
a searing wind that swept the dead before it,
but there was only silence,
only the soothing baby-blue morning
rocking me in its cradle of cumulus cloud,
only rest.
There beyond the blur of mortality,
the roots of the trees of Life and Death,
the trees William Blake called Art and Science,
joined in a kind of Gordian knot
even Alexander couldn't cut.

To me, the ideological high wire
is for fools to balance on with their illusions.
It is better to leap into the void.

Isn't that what we all want anyway?—
to eliminate all pretense
till like the oppressed who in the end
identifies with the oppressor,
we accept the worst in ourselves
and are set free.

In high school, they told me
all scientists
start from the hypothesis "what if"
and it's true.
What we as a brotherhood lack in imagination
we make up for with curiosity.
I was always motivated
by a ferocious need to know.
Can you tell me, gentlemen,
that you don't want it too?—
the public collapse,
the big fall smooth as honey down a throat.
Anything that gets you closer
to what you are.
Oh, to be born again and again
from that dark, metal womb,
the sweet, intoxicating smell of decay
the imminent dead give off
rising to embrace me.

But I could say anything, couldn't I?
Like a bed we make and unmake at whim,
the truth is always changing,
always shaped by the latest
collective urge to destroy.
So I sit here,
gnawed down by the teeth
of my nightmares.

My soul, a wound that will not heal.
All I know is that urge,
the pure, sibylline intensity of it.
Now, here at parade's end
all that matters:
our military in readiness,
our private citizens
in a constant frenzy of patriotism
and jingoistic pride,
our enemies endless,
our need to defend infinite.
Good soldiers,
we do not regret or mourn,
but pick up the guns of our fallen.

Like characters in the funny papers,
under the heading
"Further Adventures of the Lost Tribe,"
we march past the third eye of History,
as it rocks back and forth
in its hammock of stars.
We strip away the tattered fabric
of the universe
to the juicy, dark meat,
the nothing beyond time.
We tear ourselves down atom by atom,
till electron and positron,
we become our own transcendent annihilation.

ANTONIA QUINTANA PIGNO

Oppenheimer

from "La Jornada"

My two great loves are physics and New Mexico.
It's a pity they can't be combined. —J.R. Oppenheimer

Oppenheimer
I could have loved you
wrapped my legs tightly
around your white buttocks
to keep you thinly against me
without desire
     for food
      for water from mountain streams
for the journey to Jornada del Muerto
for the creation of Trinity

I would have met you along
the ridge of Frijoles Canyon
caught breathless by your intensity
and sad eyes
     your boyish dishevelment
would have seduced me
to seduce you
just clumsily enough
to surprise and charm you
away from quantum mechanics
the enigmatic half-life of identical nuclei
and the gray uniform houses of Los Alamos

at least for a while
until the 14th passed and the 15th
and the 16th
defying the test that would test us all.
Before the red dawn
I would have awakened beside you
untangled myself in that narrow bed
to slide on top of you
onto you
and whisper only for you

        mi Nuevo Méjico
Love   listen
the children are singing
as they taxi along the dirt road
back and forth on the broken bicycle.
They think they share heaven
"no tornados, no hurricanes,
we're so lucky," they say
in sing song Mexican accents
and do you know?
¿Sabes? mi Roberto
that my father couldn't stay in California
even for sweet warm thick slices
of 5¢ watermelon
pleasures of avocados
ripe oranges and lemons
right off the tree
and a steady government job
on the docks
so without word
piled us all into the Model A
the new baby born in San Francisco
and drove back to pumping gas,

fixing flats, dirt floors
and drinking cerveza with his compadres
He liked land brown
and familiar like him
afternoons burned into
the skin by sun–
his legacy to us, to me, in me.

And riding in me the passion of New Mexico
up to mountain streams and ruins without names
on the bed of an old pickup
sleeping within me the desire
to empower poetry with the very physics
of the land

Consider   querido mío

poetry—

how it changes only
perception

not the land:

A gust of wind whips a-
round the corner
of the jr high
where two girls walk
backward

whips
at their backs
lifts

                    their skirts
                            blows
                stinging sand against
                the slight curve of bare thighs
                        they chatter
                        and lick ice-cream cones
                        harbored in still coves
                            made by the slight curve
                            of slender shoulders
You could have held me by the poetry
of Classical Analysis
spoken Sanskrit verses to me
upon the ruins of the high adobe city of Puye
where ancient
we would gaze beyond Black Mesa
at the blue haze of the mountain range
ranging from the Colorado Sangre de Cristos
clear south
to the Sandías
and then, the Manzanos
but your passion was physics, the fission and fissure
of it and separation never scared you
not even my sad eyes
Don't look at me like I'm leaving you and
        your eight children
and a small kiss upon my cheek before you left
leaving me lost in crumpled linen.
I couldn't have stopped your drive through all those summers
with your family in Christ's blood red mountains
where you learned to love your version of the air
I couldn't have stopped your driven drive
past Sante Fe
Albuquerque
Isleta

Belen
slipping left
after Socorro
into the light of a new world.

ATOMIC GHOST

5. Photograph used with permission from Las Vegas News Bureau.

When the Vacation Is Over for Good

It will be strange.
Knowing at last it couldn't go on forever,
The certain voice telling us over and over
That nothing would change.

And remembering too,
Because by then it will all be done with, the way
Things were, and how we had wasted time as though
There was nothing to do,

When, in a flash
The weather turned, and the lofty air became
Unbearably heavy, the wind strikingly dumb
And our cities like ash,

And knowing also,
What we never suspected, that it was something like summer
At its most august except that the nights were warmer
And the clouds seemed to glow,

And even then,
Because we will not have changed much, wondering what
Will become of things, and who will be left to do it
All over again,

And somehow trying,
But still unable, to know just what it was
That went so completely wrong, or why it is
We are dying.

LORINE NIEDECKER

"The radio talk . . ."

The radio talk this morning
was of obliterating
the world

I notice fruit flies rise
from the rind
of the recommended
melon

WILLIAM STAFFORD

At the Bomb Testing Site

At noon in the desert a panting lizard
waited for history, its elbows tense,
watching the curve of a particular road
as if something might happen.

It was looking at something farther off
than people could see, an important scene
acted in stone for little selves
at the flute end of consequences.

There was just a continent without much on it
under a sky that never cared less.
Ready for a change, the elbows waited.
The hands gripped hard on the desert.

GARY SNYDER

Vapor Trails

Twin streaks twice higher than cumulus,
Precise plane icetracks in the vertical blue
Cloud-flaked light-shot shadow-arcing
Field of all future war, edging off to space.

Young expert U.S. pilots waiting
The day of criss-cross rockets
And white blossoming smoke of bomb,
The air world torn and staggered for these
Specks of brushy land and ant-hill towns—

    I stumble on the cobble rockpath
Passing through temples,
Watching for two-leaf pine
    —spotting that design.

N

"Operation Redwing" in the Pacific, 1956. Seventeen
nuclear detonations of large hydrogen weapons.
Colonel Langston Harrison
of the u.s. Air Force's 4926th Squadron
piloted one of twenty-five various aircraft sent in
soon after the explosions
to "make repeated and protracted penetration"
of the mushroom clouds: no special protection,
no procedures for decontamination.
Officially labeled "Human
experiment number 133," under direction
of Los Alamos. Even miles away, even chickens
who turned away & closed their eyes, saw their own
& others' bones. In the clouds, Langston
whistled at the green aura around his B-57,
the lighter green diffusion of sequins within.

Later, limited compensation to civilian populations,
not for the vanished deities of their lagoons,
or their altered genes, or their unborn
or stillborn children, not for proliferation
of cancers for generations, but for eminent domain.

No recognition for most "atomic veterans"
whose records show a few rems of radiation,
who ate 100—all this forseen by American technicians
making rational decisions, even warning patriotic skeletons
to remain unknown, even experimental plutonium injections,

the touch of Belsen, engines run
by brains gone into irradiated green,
these lines of translucent skin, this sound begun
at the back of the throat, closed in
with the tip of the tongue,

N.

Mushroom Clouds

   During the final minutes of the raid
Miss Nurvak made us kneel with our heads buried
between our knees—the blast that ruined our lives
was her yardstick breaking in half and confetti
she shredded over us was fallout. One boy threw up
Cheerios beneath his desk and then ran from class
with wet pants. The rest of us survived the drill
for milk and cookies during Miss Nurvak's nightmare
sermon on the Red Menace.

   Miss Nurvak,
who said we had nothing to fear but fear itself,
was scared half-to-death. The shelter beneath her garden
was stocked with canned goods and sterilized water,
rations against the coming days of radioactive ash.
In gas mask and green fatigues, Miss Nurvak
would needlepoint and listen to the gramophone
until the fatal firestorms passed and she raised
her periscope, searching for pupils
from the lost second-grade.

   So life was more serious than I thought.
And it was Miss Nurvak who made me want to be a man
as hard and strong as the stone man on the stallion
in the park, the general with epaulets of pigeon shit.
I imagined myself in crash helmet and bulletproof vest,
Miss Nurvak's periscope rising from the blackened grass:
how happy she would be to see a successful graduate
of Central Elementary who had not been reduced to ash,
whose ideals had not been shaken by the atomic blast,
who pushed the culprit forward with his bayonet,
a boy with wet pants.

DIANE GLANCY

Harry S Truman Library, Independence, Missouri

Your birth to a mule-trader in 1884
wasn't much noticed.
No more than the large hole in the cloud
the morning of your death.
But a photographer for the *Kansas City Star*
waiting at the hospital
saw it when he left
and we read it in the news,
Heaven Opens to Receive a Leader.

It seems there was always an opening for you.
After you failed in the clothing business
you went into politics:
County Judge, u.s. Senator, Vice President.
You whistle-stopped your way
from Missouri to the White House with Bess
on the B&O.

In your library
Margaret's silver fork & spoon,
her doll's shoes, jacks,
a little stove with an electrical cord.

In pictures
women in large-heeled black shoes
and hats with veils
listen to your *Missouri Waltz*
on the White House piano.

They wave their handkerchiefs
at the 1950 Lincoln where you sat
with your two radios and two heaters.

In your library
your briefcase and letters.
Your convention memorabilia:
a *Truman is Human* campaign button,
flags, ballot box,
a matchbook with a mule on the cover.

Then down the hall
we finally get to it.
A Japanese doll given to you in 1950
not five years after the bomb.

We walk silently past the display case
wondering why some are blessed
with a hole in a cloud
while others watched a bomb under a parachute
they first thought was food for American captives.
And even after the sparkle of white light
some still didn't know
the blossoms that fell from the sky
were from a kimono 25 kilometers away.

In the gentle library
it's hard to imagine black rain,
a burning ring around the sun,
blistered flesh draped from bodies,
vomit, diarrhea.
Some going insane,
others crying for death.

But you, Harry, carried on,
tough buzzard that you were.
Leader of our country.

You were in Washington the years
I walked to school over leaves
that crumpled under my feet.
My father in a bulky overcoat and fedora
waving, smiling,
backed our car from the drive,
the heater rattling like grease that popped
from burning bodies,
or the leaves from trees
that lined the drive of the White House
and my schoolroom window.

In your library
there's a replica of your Oval Office
with a ceiling like the cloud that opened
the morning of your death.
There's a mule-shoe on your desk,
a sexy picture of Margaret,
a black telephone that rang that morning
of August 6th.

DAVID RAY

For Harry S Truman in Hell

Your rusty Chrysler was advertised in the *K.C. Star.*
I called but was put off by the five thousand price
though the man admitted chickens had roosted in it
three decades and he had only lately found out you owned it,
drove it to the store a few times and in a parade.
I'd always hated you because you said you'd lost no sleep
over those children of Hiroshima, then sent the bombers back
to wipe out Nagasaki and yet I admired your desk-top phrase
THE BUCK STOPS HERE, and your unflappable sweet smirk,
rivalled by those great ones, Jimmy Stewart, Glenn Ford, Henry
    Fonda.
Once I took my mother and her retired army cook husband
to your museum where were displayed all
those presents you got as President, including
golden tea service from the Shah and a Turkey carpet hung
across a wall and well-lit, and down the hall
endless movies were shown in a little theatre—
your campaign whistle stops back when we had trains
with black balconies on their rears. Buxom Bess
was with you and you were unpretentious, just an average
guy from Missouri, the Show Me State. In the White House
you played just one tune on the piano, *Missouri Waltz.*
Once Lauren Bacall sat above you with legs crossed
while you grinned. By then we boys in backyards
had mourned FDR, had heard over the radio his caisson roll.
TV was still a fantasy—that ancient crone
who kept ten parrots told us they'd show her pictures soon
on the radio, soon as the war was done. She pointed to
two loose wires where they'd hook it up but we were sure
she was the fool with two wires loose. But neither would

our high school brains have grasped
that men with good minds stood in the desert, placed their bets
on whether they would blow the planet up or just New Mexico.
Therefore once when no one looked I stood above your grave
and thought I should be Gulliver, who put out fires with pee
in Lilliput—for I thought I saw the fires of Hiroshima
rage still in grass near your giant stone, saw frozen shadows
of those thousands just as they were caught forever
in the concrete of five bridges spanning the River Kyobashi.
But the F.B.I. watched, no doubt: *this* was *their* sacred spot.
Strange world! A man can go to jail for pissing on a grave
and yet a *great* one murders thousands, no penalty at all,
not for you who sent a naked man screaming with his eyeball
in his hand, who blackened thousands, tore breasts off
a beauty so they bled like pomegranates. Children nursed
their mothers' corpses to drink the milk of death.
Hair of the streetcar dead stood straight from fear.
A hand uplifted burned with blue flames through its fingers.
A squad of soldiers marching became a little ash and trickling
    flakes.
Through whorls of fire the black rain fell. And you were proud
as if good deeds would never end and we who followed
would praise your name and hold it sacred in our hearts.
"For Harry S Truman in Hell" I loft my amber arc
and defy the authorities. Out of the hole
in your bronze fingers your admirers again and again
steal your walking cane of Missouri willow.
And again and again it's replaced at public expense.

The Hell Mural: Panel I

Iri and Toshi Maruki are "painting the bomb."
Their painting, they say, will comfort the souls of the dead.
"It's a dreadful cruel scene of great beauty,"
Toshi says. "The face may be deformed but there's kindness
in a finger or a breast, even in hell."
The Hell Mural spreads over the floor.

Iri stretches naked on the floor,
painting. He remembers Hiroshima after the bomb—
the bodies stacked up, arms outstretched toward hell,
nothing he could see that was not dead,
nothing that cared at all for human kindness,
nothing that wept at such terror, such beauty.

Now a brush stroke here, a thick wash there, and beauty
writhes and stretches from the canvas floor.
He wants his art to "collaborate with kindness,"
he wants his art to "uncover the bomb."
But no lifetime's enough to paint all the dead
or put all those who belong there in hell.

"Hitler and Truman," he says, "of course are in hell.
But even those of us who live for beauty
are in hell, no less so than the dead."
(He paints himself and Toshi on the floor.)
"All of us who cannot stop the bomb
are now in hell. It's no kindness

to say different. It's no kindness
to insist on heaven; there's only hell."

Toshi adds bees and maggots to the bomb,
and birds, cats, her pregnant niece, the beauty
of severed breast and torn limb on the killing floor.
"In Hiroshima," she says, "we crossed a river on the dead

bodies stacked up like a bridge. Now the dead
souls must be comforted with kindness.
Come, walk in your socks across our floor,
walk on the canvas. (A little dirt in hell
almost improves it.) Can you see the beauty
of this torso, that ear lobe, this hip bone of the bomb?"

Iri and Toshi Maruki, in "Hell," are painting the bomb,
the mural on their floor alive with the thriving dead.
Come walk on their kindness, walk on their troublesome beauty.

JOHN BALABAN

Atomic Ghost

As our plane droned south to Peoria
all the cattle ponds and creeks below
caught sun, flared bright, then faded
back into smog seeping from Chicago,
so that looking west through oval ports
you saw jags of water wink and flash.

Then the sky ballooned with light so bright
the firmament bucked and our plane
dropped like a long sigh through the magnetized air
and the woman who ordered a Bloody Mary
swirled in her seat, a small cyclone of ash
saying syllables of smoke in the whirligig fire.

Almost at once, cells quirked and recombined.
In the company of scorched ant and armadillo
new lives shuffled forth, sick in their seed,
irradiated, wracked with lunatic genes.
Queer things issued from monsters of the past
as earth reassessed the error that was man,
that was me, my wife, our child. All
entered the pall of incinerated air.

Oh, to be cast from the Garden again and forever.

GARY SNYDER

Strategic Air Command

The hiss and flashing lights of a jet
Pass near Jupiter in Virgo.
He asks, how many satellites in the sky?
Does anyone know where they all are?
What are they doing, who watches them?

Frost settles on the sleeping bags.
The last embers of fire,
One more cup of tea,
At the edge of a high lake rimmed with snow.

These cliffs and the stars
Belong to the same universe.
This little air in between
Belongs to the twentieth century and its wars.

What the End Is For

(Grand Forks, North Dakota)

A boy just like you took me out to see them,
    the five hundred B-52s on alert on the runway,
fully loaded fully manned pointed in all the directions,
    running every minute
of every day.
    They sound like a sickness of the inner ear,

where the heard foams up into the noise of listening,
    where the listening arrives without being extinguished.
The huge hum soaks up into the dusk.
    The minutes spring open. Six is too many.
From where we watch,
    from where even watching is an anachronism,

from the 23d of March from an open meadow,
    the concertina wire on its double helix
designed to tighten round a body if it turns
    is the last path the sun can find to take out,
each barb flaring gold like a braille being read,
    then off with its knowledge and the sun
is gone. . . .

That's when the lights on all the extremities, like an outline like a
    dress,
    become loud in the story,
and a dark I have not seen before
    sinks in to hold them one
by one.

Strange plot made to hold so many inexhaustible
screams.
Have you ever heard in a crowd mutterings of
blame

that will not modulate that will not rise?
He tells me, your stand-in, they *stair-step* up.
He touches me to have me look more deeply
in
to where for just a moment longer
color still lives:
the belly white so that it looks like sky, the top
some kind of brown, some soil—How does it look

from up there now
this meadow we lie on our bellies in, this field Iconography
tells me stands for sadness
because the wind can move through it uninterrupted?
What is it the wind
would have wanted to find and didn't

leafing down through this endless admiration unbroken
because we're too low for it
to find us?
Are you still there for me now in that dark
we stood in for hours
letting it sweep as far as it could down over us
unwilling to move, irreconcilable? What *he*
wants to tell me,

his whisper more like a scream
over this eternity of engines never not running,
is everything: how the crews assigned to each plane
for a week at a time, the seven boys, must live
inseparable,

how they stay together for life,
how the wings are given a life of
   seven feet of play,

how they drop practice bombs called *shapes* over Nevada,
   how the measures for counterattack in air
have changed and we
   now forego firepower for jamming, for the throwing
of false signals. The meadow, the meadow hums, love, with the
   planes,
   as if every last blade of grass where wholly possessed

by this practice, wholly prepared. The last time I saw you,
   we stood facing each other as dusk came on.
I leaned against the refrigerator, you leaned against the door.
   The picture window behind you was slowly extinguished,
the tree went out, the two birdfeeders, the metal braces on them.
   The light itself took a long time,

bits in puddles stuck like the useless
   splinters of memory, the chips
of history, hopes, laws handed down. *Here, hold these* he says, these
   grasses these
torn pods, he says, smiling over the noise another noise, *take these*
   he says, my hands wrong for

the purpose, here,
   not-visible-from-the-sky, prepare yourself with these, boy and
bouquet of
   thistleweed and wort and william and
timothy. We stood there. Your face went out a long time
   before the rest of it. Can't see you anymore I said. *Nor I,*
you, whatever you still were
   replied.
When I asked you to hold me you refused.
   When I asked you to cross the six feet of room to hold me

you refused. Until I
    couldn't rise out of the patience either any longer
to make us
    take possession.
Until we were what we must have wanted to be:
    shapes the shapelessness was taking back.
Why should I lean out?
    Why should I move?
When the Maenads tear Orpheus limb from limb,
    they throw his head

out into the river.
    Unbodied it sings
all the way downstream, all the way to the single ocean,
    head floating in current downriver singing,
until the sound of the cataracts grows,
    until the sound of the open ocean grows and the voice.

Directions for Carrying Explosive Nuclear Wastes through Metropolitan New York

Enter the Long Island Expressway at Brookhaven.
Proceed West. Exit at Hoyt Street in Astoria.
Turn left onto Astoria Boulevard. Trundle
under the elevated tracks there. Turn
right to ramp for the 59th Street Bridge.
Cross the Bridge. Follow local streets traveling
West until Amsterdam Avenue. At Amsterdam
turn right. Proceed North.

Special Note to Drivers of Trucks Carrying
Explosive Nuclear Waste through
Metropolitan New York:

Check oil levels every five miles.
Change fan belt every thousand.
Check tire pressure every morning.
Change tires.
Buy radials.
Check shocks every fifty miles.
Change shocks every hundred.
Check rearview mirror and sideview mirror
incessantly.
Keep eyes on road.
Grant all other vehicles and each pedestrian
the right of way.

Do not pass.
Do not drive in the rain.
Do not drive in the snow.
Do not drive in the dark.
Signal.
Use headlights on high beam.
Go slow.
Do not brake suddenly or
otherwise.
Think about your mother
and look out for the crazies.

Tar

The first morning of Three Mile Island: those first disquieting, un-
certain, mystifying hours.
All morning a crew of workmen have been tearing the old decrepit
roof off our building,
and all morning, trying to distract myself, I've been wandering out
to watch them
as they hack away the leaden layers of asbestos paper and disassemble
the disintegrating drains.
After half a night of listening to the news, wondering how to know
a hundred miles downwind
if and when to make a run for it and where, then a coming bolt
awake at seven
when the roofers we've been waiting for since winter sent their lad-
ders shrieking up our wall,
we still know less than nothing: the utility company continues
making little of the accident,
the slick federal spokesmen still have their evasions in some sem-
blance of order.
Surely we suspect now we're being lied to, but in the meantime,
there are the roofers,
setting winch-frames, sledging rounds of tar apart, and there I am,
on the curb across, gawking.

I never realized what brutal work it is, how matter-of-factly and
harrowingly dangerous.
The ladders flex and quiver, things skid from the edge, the materi-
als are bulky and recalcitrant.
When the rusty, antique nails are levered out, their heads pull off;
the under-roofing crumbles.

Even the battered little furnace, roaring along as patient as a donkey, chokes and clogs,

a dense, malignant smoke shoots up, someone has to fiddle with a cock, then hammer it,

before the gush and stench will deintensify, the dark, Dantean broth wearily subside.

In its crucible, the stuff looks bland, like licorice, spill it, though, on your boots or coveralls,

it sears, and everything is permeated with it, the furnace gunked with burst and half-burst bubbles,

the men themselves so completely slashed and mucked they seem almost from another realm, like trolls.

When they take their break, they leave their brooms standing at attention in the asphalt pails,

work gloves clinging like Brer Rabbit to the bitten shafts, and they slouch along the precipitous lip,

the enormous sky behind them, the heavy noontime air alive with shimmers and mirages.

Sometime in the afternoon I had to go inside: the advent of our vigil was upon us.

However much we didn't want to, however little we would do about it, we'd understood:

we were going to perish of all this, if not now, then soon, if not soon, then someday.

Someday, some final generation, hysterically aswarm beneath an atmosphere as unrelenting as rock,

would rue us all, anathematize our earthly comforts, curse our surfeits and submissions.

I think I know, though I might rather not, why my roofers stay so clear to me and why the rest,

the terror of that time, the reflexive disbelief and distancing, all we should hold on to, dims so.

I remember the president in his absurd protective booties, looking absolutley unafraid, the fool.

I remember a woman on the front page glaring across the misty
   Susquehanna at those looming stacks.
But, more vividly, the men, silvered with glitter from the shingles,
   clinging like starlings beneath the eaves.
Even the leftover carats of tar in the gutter, so black they seemed
   to suck the light out of air.
By nightfall kids had come across them: every sidewalk on the
   block was scribbled with obscenities and hearts.

GARY METRAS

Utilities Advertisement in the Wake of Three Mile Island

(a found poem)

We are committed to candor and openness.
It may not be possible to answer all the questions.

Incident. Core material. Meltdown.

This is a time to avoid emotionalism.
Truth only gets obscured
and rational decisions are impeded.

Leak. Emissions. Exposure.

There are lessons to be learned.
First consideration goes to public
safety and health.
Look at our record.

For radiation consider
x-rays, microwaves, the sun.

This is a matter of risk assessment.
No available energy source
is risk-free.
The question of human error must be dealt with.

It may not be possible.
We are committed.

JEFFREY HILLARD

The Message

I want the sign to read, *never come back again.*
Instead, it reads, *Safety Is A Man's Best Friend.*
I know each one: *Alert!* above the utility room.
Know Your Goggles near the loading docks.
I have partners who can't spell half the words,
each orange letter a directive that keeps our
sleeves buttoned and hard-hats within reach.
A mishmash of phrases that exalt our lungs
above any skill; words bold as hot metal,
composed in some super's office, under a cool fan.
They'll never convince me that I'd burn myself
or remove my gloves near a blasting furnace
or breathe the fumes from a lead vat
rimmed with sulfuric acid.

I don't need signs to echo my flaws.
A Careless Employee Is A Disaster In Uniform.
I already load sludge and leave my body
to the eyes of a detector scanner.
Since I drive a forklift, I look ahead,
not above. Today, something is different.
I imagine the tar-black walls swelling,
tiers of sludge frothing over the catwalks,
my lead shield coming apart, dust floating past.

I salvage my thoughts, especially after lunch.
I know it's dangerous, but I'll steer the lift
near a pit and join a crew for a cigarette.
We take three puffs, crush them on our hard-hats
and drop them in a shirt pocket. Safe, not sorry.

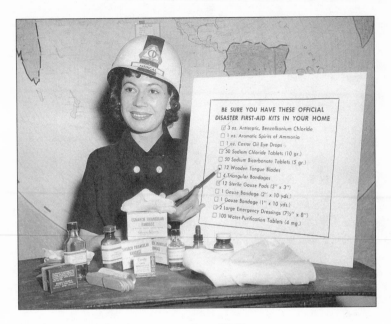

6. Photograph used with permission from UPI/Bettmann

I'm not yet relieved. I imagine another sign
saying, *All bodily cells replenished here,*
but the wisdom I receive is *Shower Thoroughly.*
I find a blessing in each thump of the time-clock,
in the exit gate, in the sign whose broken letters
remind us to dump uniforms in the black barrel.
I say to no one in particular, *I do, I do.*
I think, what else can I give? What else
do they want from a man whose name is duty
and paycheck, a man who sheds these clothes
like they're footprints to be mopped and forgotten.

MARY JO SALTER

Chernobyl

Once upon a time,
the word alone was scary.
Now, quainter than this rhyme,
it's the headline of a story

long yellowed in the news.
The streets were hosed in Kiev,
and Poles took more shampoos.
The evacuees were brave.

Under the gay striped awning
of Europe's common market,
half-empty booths were yawning
at the small change in the pocket.

As far away as Rome,
unseen through weeks of sun,
the cloud kept children home.
Milk gurgled down the drain.

In Wales, spring lambs were painted
blue, not to be eaten
till the next spring when . . . Still tainted,
they'd grown into blue mutton.

Then we had had enough.
Fear's harder to retain
than hope or indifference. Safe
and innocent, the rain

fell all night as we slept,
and the story at last was dead—
all traces of it swept
under the earth's green bed.

SUJATA BHATT

Wine from Bordeaux

Today I've invented a man
who has bought two thousand bottles
of a 1985 wine from Bordeaux,
the *Bois-Malot* which won
the Bronze Medal in 1986.
And now this 1985 *Bois-Malot* has become
even better than gold, and it will stay
good, it will delight you
    for years to come.

Over here, in Ostertor
you and I would have to pay
about *vierzehn Mark* for a bottle.
But I'm sure my imaginary man
has worked out some special deal
with the shopkeepers, maybe even
with the people
    who planted the grapes.

He's bought two thousand bottles already
and plans to buy more.

1985 is the year
before Chernobyl.

He doesn't like
to ingest anything harvested
    in Europe after 1985.

"This wine goes very well
with New Zealand lamb,"
he confides to the wine shop owner.
"It's the only meat
I feel safe eating . . ." he whispers.

No doubt
he's got a large cellar
to hoard all those bottles
of crimson Bordeaux
with their handsome brown labels.
I imagine him smiling
at their sharp dark winks—
    rows and rows of rounded shadows
each time he opens the door.

There's another man
I can tell you about.
He is real.
He got himself sterilized
in May 1986 when he was eighteen
because he was convinced
his chromosomes were damaged.
And he didn't want to pass on
    any mistakes.

While the women
who gave birth over here
in 1986 sometimes didn't know
    what to eat.

I imagine some of them still
scrutinize their children
with fear, wishing they could supervise
the health of every cell.

While in the towns near Chernobyl
embryos didn't make it
fetuses didn't make it
and the babies who managed
to get born and who managed to grow
into children—suddenly
become sick with leukemia.

But the child
that I still think of
was one eight-year-old boy
who loved playing in the sand
      like most children
who didn't notice dirt or mud on his clothes
      like most children—

But then he started begging
to be allowed to take a shower
whenever he came indoors
thinking the water
      thinking the water would wash
          it all off—

Eight-Legged Colt, Chernobyl

After photographs in *Time*

Its lower jaw scissors
sideways as it whinnies
and struggles to rise

tuber legs flopping
and flailing, hooves
striking air, ground

it propels itself, almost
as if it were running.
Try to forget

the eager cast of its eyes,
its black velvet
body thrashing up

wisps of dirt.
And sympathy, horror,
the adulterated

facts of its birth—
it knows nothing
but the purest

urge to find footing
even as it drags
itself, through

the spring
weeds and back
into the earth.

Radiophobia

Is this only fear of radiation?
Or rather, fear of wars?
Perhaps the dread of betrayal,
cowardice, stupidity, anarchy?
It's time to sort out
radiophobia.
It is—
when those who've gone through the tragedy of Chernobyl
refuse to submit
to the truths of government ministers
("Here, you swallow exactly this much today!").
We will not be resigned
to falsified ciphers,
malevolent thoughts,
however you brand us.
We don't wish—and do not suggest it!—
to view the world through a bureaucrat's glasses.
We're too suspicious.
And we remember each victim
as a brother.
Now we look out on a fragile Earth
through the panes of abandoned buildings.
These glasses no longer deceive us—
These glasses show us more clearly—
believe me—
the shrinking rivers,
poisoned forests,
infants born not to survive . . .
Mighty uncles, what have you given them
beyond television bravado?

How marvelously children absorbed
radiation, once thought so hazardous!
(Adults suffer from radiophobia—
for kids is it still "adaptation"?)
What has become of the world
if the most humane of professions
has also turned bureaucratic?
Radiophobia,
may you be omnipresent!
Not waiting until additional jolts,
new misfortunes,
have transformed more thousands
who survived the inferno
into seers—
Radiophobia might cure the world
of negligence, greed and glut,
bureaucratism and spiritual void,
so that, through somebody's good intentions,
we do not mutate into non-humankind.

> translated from the Russian
> by Leonid Levin and Elisavietta Ritchie

Note: "Radiophobia" was the term used by Soviet authorities to dismiss the
physical suffering or illness of those exposed to Chernobyl's radiation as
merely symptoms of fear.

MAUREEN HURLEY

Country of Origin

The first hunters who crossed Siberia
survived winter's ancestors
because they wasted nothing—
something of the Inuit remains.
What do we know of Siberia?
We say Siberia, naming the nameless zone
between the *taiga* and the tundra.
We say it because it conjures up the idea of wind and snow
unfettered by man to come and go where it pleases.
When we say Siberia the air fills with tundra flowers
and we mean the Siberia of stunted pines
and caribou migrations, but it's also the Siberia
of strip mines and nuclear physics.
We say it midsummer, under a curtain of fire,
where night never begins;
and in winter, where it never stops.
We say it to sustain us as the invisible wolf
testing the strength of double-paned glass
stares in from the pupiled eye of night.
We say Siberia, stretching out syllables
until it becomes the wind's voice.
Sigh-bier-ria.
We say it as a punishment to our children.
We will ship them off to Siberia.
Banishment is always another country.
We make jokes about it,
and so I touch your golden skin in summer,
how it radiates the sun
while mine is the white of winter.
In the land of exile,

the land of the long ruble,
of opportunists and political prisoners,
where does the Siberian tiger sleep now?
We say Siberia and know nothing about it.

You tell me someone has to be the first
to love across political boundaries
until nations put down their ideals.
There's little comfort in knowing tears or blood
are the same chemistry as their mother, the ocean.
In Novosibirsk, scientists in white rooms
play nuclear physics with God—
like ours at White Sands and Alamagordo.
Something of the landscape must touch them—
surely they dream?
Last night, the sky wore red
and I stood between two rainbows.
Prisms and physics could not explain away refracted light.
There are those desperate enough to drink perfume.
They must've pissed the very heart of summer flowers into snow
only to go blind, was it worth it? *Nosdrov'yeh,*
a toast clawing olfactory nerves and tissue—
the period between midwinter and spring. *Asylum.*
But you've been there too, a spy among inmates,
your drawings record far better than any camera
life within the walls of insanity—who's more insane:
the Georgian man over and over again in pencil,
the scientists who turn their backs on the earth,
or those who send the flower of their youth
to front lines to bathe in jellied gasoline
in the name of an idea?
We are all crazy.
It comes with the territory.

Did I tell you Solzhenitsyn lives in a fortress
of his own choosing, deep in the mountains of Vermont?
It's the *Gulag* all over again.
He brought his Siberian islands with him.
Dogs patrol the electric fence in regimented intervals.
Stalin's been dead nearly as many years as we've lived.
America is also an experiment,
an armed song singing itself
toward extinction like all the rest.
Yes, we are victims of history—
fill the silos with grain.
But I touch your face,
my fingers memorize geography.
You ask, *How does it feel to be living with bears?*
Everyone loses their teeth in Siberia
and you never met a woman who bites.
I cannot forget your eyes—all that blue,
not of glaciers and ice but of the soft secret heart of stone.
Translucence leashed and folded like linen bedsheets.
Your hand reaches for the moon hidden beneath my shirt,
seeking familiar patterns in a gesture that's timeless.
Learning to live with the land is something the Inuit knew
but even they've begun to turn their backs on it.
We should be around the fire telling stories,
buried in thick furs, safe in each other's arms
but we're not dressed in skins.
I carry a bear's tooth in my pocket
and keep skulls outside my window, just in case.
We live on opposite sides of the earth,
lovers in exile, but love is like that.
We need visas and annulments.
By naming it, it's too late,
we're no longer in the country of origin.
Siberia is singing from the heart of deepest night.

Small hooves pound in our chests.
We live on blubber,
savor fatty tissue and cannot sleep.
V'kusna? Out of death comes life;
from life, death follows like wolves
trailing the caribou herd.

JACK MARSHALL

In the Shadow of the Poisoned Wind

In Arctic latitudes, almost another
planet, Laplanders herd their radiation-
laden reindeer down from their mountain

feeding grounds. Without a sound now
they glide like robes of royalty, billowing, breathing
sleeves of vapor, tiara antlers, thick

fur glowing dark as mahogany
fattened on vegetation watered by nuclear rains.
To be slaughtered, and not eaten. So we

go into what has been gliding
forward to meet us from so long ago
we have seen coming against the black

velvet of galactic space,
the many pouring down to the one
wave not yet broken. Shadow

on ice, here and gone.

Waiting for the Invasion

In other years I watched the sky for birds
flying south in formation.
This year they pass in unbroken lines through my sleep,
driven down on machine wings.

I know the voice you use
for telling the children not to fear
every droning sound
that scatters their play like shrapnel or shattered
ice across asphalt; every approach sends them
into piles of human limbs under trucks,
sends the youngest under your breasts
that ache like the unmilked she-goat bleating somewhere,
ache with the waiting.

Every child waited for death angels: I
listened at night for the Russians, who would
know our little town
by its twin water towers.
Someone, believe this, painted the towers black
hoping to save us.
And even now, fear is a night-time animal,
winged engines pulsing and the drone
of my mother praying
in the bed where she never died.

No one slipped through a lake of night sky
in search of our secret towers.
No one. I know this now, but some believed
and believing still, prepare the massacre.

LATE SPRING IN THE NUCLEAR AGE

7. Photograph used with permission from Los Alamos National Laboratory.

ANDREW HUDGINS

Late Spring in the Nuclear Age

For Clare Rossini

The fish hit water nymphs, breaking surface.
I hear the splash but when I turn to look
it's gone, the troubled water smoothing itself
back into blue glass. But sometimes I see it,
a bass wrench in midair as it pierces
the membrane of our world. How graceless it is,
the absolute half-second of its flight.

It's hard to say what's different.
It's not the bass. It's not that
I've seen two butterflies poised on one leaf,
their moist wings drying with slow rhythmic flaps.
The leaf quavered beneath their double weight.
Nor that above me on the hill I hear
a small boy hunting in the cemetery.
A hummingbird dissolves in the shotgun blast.
In water oaks the sparrows pause, don't sing,
then one by one their voices catch, unfurl,
as if they had forgotten what they heard.
But that is nothing new. We're used to death—
if not resigned. I stretch here on the damp grass,
a paste of seeds and dew smeared on my boots,
trying to move the world into my mind
so I'll have it when summer settles in,
when it's too hot for blossom-set or talk
and nothing moves. This is what's different:
my prayer there'll be a summer to survive,
that our deaths will not be the last.

JAMES GRABILL

The Lightning

It is the time's discipline to think of the death of all living, and yet live.
—Wendell Berry

Like you, I have looked off the cliff
of life forms and have seen ants on the rock,
and I have heard locusts in the harvested trees.
I have stood like a grave against war,
the months swinging on a hinge of exchange
in such a universe that lets us go.
                                        I look up
from the sidewalk: massive nuclear blast lighting
everywhere total destruction into blank void
for eternity! Then there are buildings as before,
neighborhoods, people and animals, in this moment
we are alive, breathing in such a universe development
that machinery grows and locks into fuel warfare
of basements to golden-winged Christ heavens
we were promised for after the shift of truck gears
slamming shut to where we will live in the castles
of perfection, with the undead families,
and the undead beings of all time flashing
as one?, in a cathedral of the rising sun
and setting sun at once?, breathing eternity
into the tiniest plasm or twinge near where worms slip
their lost train of where the void stops twisting
and excreting lubrication,
                                        as only the supreme
maker could fit it into an individual bird
or dog energy, not only a species, but an individual,

then another individual and another. And what happens
when a person we live beside falls off the earth?
I look up, toward the shipyards. It is a split
second, atomic war, life as we see it, atomic war,
life as we see it, atomic war, life as we see it.

EDWINA TRENTHAM

Hurricane Season

For Ben

When I was a Bermudian child
September was always a promise—
dark sunlit days of oil smooth breakers
rolling silently into the shore,
deep turquoise refusing to reflect
the charcoal sky—and I recall just

what to do. Close the shutters, but leave
one window cracked on the lee. Hide all
garbage cans and wicker furniture
from the wind's clatter. And always make
sure everyone is in the house long
before the hurricane hits its stride.

This one has no season, no sure signs,
though I find myself scanning the sweet
blue overhead too often—dreaming
those dark, lazy arcs of extinction—
and, oh Ben, the pamphlet you brought home
from school is quick to say exactly

what to do in an emergency.
Stay in the house. Close doors and windows.
Don't eat any food from your garden.
Don't use furnaces, fireplaces—
they draw air inside. And above all,
don't try to gather your family.

It's late. Our forsythia has lost
the scarlet cardinal, a half-moon howls
lopsided in blue turned slate, and I have spent
the day trying to imagine not
trying to find you.

JANA HARRIS

Dream of the Hair-Burning Smell

the women gather, their dreams
played back again and again:

will the children be heirs
to the cloud passing over

killing everyone?
in the day, her eyes open

one smells her own hair burning,
another says, after the cloud

a flesh-sweat falling
from her face, her arms

her daughter's forehead dissolving
when she awoke, she wondered

how will I kill my little girl?
these dreams, they say

oh, these dreams
of row crop corn smoke-stained,

the silks burnt away,
another does not in her dream

see the fire, just
the burning smell of hair

of corn husks, the smell
of the false prophet

is everywhere in their dreams,
in the end, black ash

is what rises up again,
these dreams, they say

oh, these dreams

Spuyten Duyvil

The bridge between the Bronx and Manhattan crosses a small body of water which runs between the Hudson and the East River and is called Spuyten Duyvil, Dutch for "the devil's tail."

I.

A computer chip malfunctions. A micro-
scopic switch slips. You can cut an apple into

quarters. East of the Urals, a technician
sweats into gray fatigues. In Nevada

a video screen registers activity.
The President carries a briefcase called

the football. His men sit at a small table
or cluster in easy chairs watching a screen

tick with revelation. You adjust your
blinds. I flip a cellar switch. A terrorist

monitors the football. A red light on a red
telephone flashes. The technician cues

his superior. Afternoon in the desert.
Dead of night in the Urals. Rockets

surge from concrete silos like lipsticks sprung
from gargantuan tubes. I have seen bridges

dynamited in 3-D color, mushroom clouds
engorge and shrivel in 4/4 time, faces

of children etched with acid to rippling
wound on screens the size of footballs.

So have you. In a cellar where the ceiling is
low, I bump my head, shatter the only source

of light. This cellar was not built airtight,
but I keep firewood here, my water pump, boiler.

II.

I am driving across the bridge
which connects the Bronx to

Manhattan, river blue below, sun
rippling its surprising expanse

and always entering New York
by this route, I love life.

Planes. No, missiles. Or must we
call them warheads? How fast?

Morning: You stand at your kitchen
telephone then drive down the hill.

Or twilight: You bend at a keyboard
moving as you play. Ten minutes

from that place to this. Frozen
expression on the face of

the drunk who wipes my windshield
on the Bowery. I want your

hand. Warheads. You slip an apple,
quarter by quarter, into your mouth.

We never sat facing each other:
What might we make of this love?

III.

Anyone who calls a broken heart
a metaphor hasn't seen the crack

in this sunset, fire clouds parting,
cylindrical beasts roaring

toward us. Do they land? Or do objects
tumble blazing, each from an open

hatch? Sudden light so bright
it brings utter darkness. Sound so loud

it could be silence. I am blind and
I step from my car. My hair is

on fire. It could be an earring
or an orange pinwheel. My hand is

burning. My hair stinks when it
burns. Below this bridge at the tip of

the city is a white sand beach. Did you
know that? Tell me, why don't you

reach for my hand? We are all blind, all
feel heat which mounts so fast

I can't tell if I sweat or shiver.

IV.

My hair has burned back to my
scalp and now my skin is

burning off my brain. Flesh melts
down my leg like syrup. We

won't walk to the river. There's
no mirror and my head is too hot

to touch. The birds are
burning. They say cities will melt

like fat. That one has fewer bones.
Breathe? He was just collecting

our quarters. We were dancing. They
told me this would happen:

Hot oceans, flat darkness.
I stay awake to speak this:

My fingers have burned to bone and so
have yours. I never wanted a child,

but I saved everything important
so those who came after could learn.

V.

It has not been explained to us that
a computer chip has the shape of

a wafer but is invisible to the
naked eye or that a switch has less

thickness than a capillary or that
the cloud of fire is as fierce and huge as

Niagara Falls. You have chosen
this distance: We will not hear

the terrible news together. When they
tell us we have the power to stop this,

we speak only of our powerlessness
to stop a blizzard in April. There is

nothing more I could have said to you.
You cross the Golden Gate. Planes?

No, missiles. How fast? None of the
children believe they will be

grandparents. Those behind bars will burn
behind bars and I think of flowers. Why

doesn't this scare me as much as losing
love again or not having enough

money? I will break a bone or my bones
will burn. I can't see what's happening

in Nevada. I keep giving them money.
You're not here. My breath

is burning. We must go downstairs, take
hands with the others, speak something.

VI.

When they said put your head to the wall,
fold your arms behind your neck, I was

not afraid. Even when I saw the movies,
I wasn't afraid, but I am afraid of

burning, of burning and breaking. When
they say we will burn, I feel knives. When

they say buildings will fly apart, that
I will be crushed by a concrete buttress or

a steel beam, I hear the weeping of
everyone into whose eyes I have been

afraid to look. If men carried knives
in airplanes, this is how it would be:

Airplanes are silver. They fly across the sky
which is blue. One day a hatch falls open,

knives fly down like rain, and we are all cut
and all bleed. What if, day after day,

knives fell from the sky? I would go into my
cellar, hope my roof would repel knives.

Failure of love has brought us to this.

VII.

You iron. It could be thunder. They keep
listening to music. Let me tell you, the

difference is the whole city is an
oven which won't go out, and if it could

there would be no one to put it out.
Let me tell you, you will never

see morning again or early spring. Look,
fire sheets down the river like wind

before a hurricane. Listen, it rushes
through city streets like falls down a mountain.

No one will read what you write. No one will
eat what you put on the table. It is not

thunder. There is no time to make amends.
You will not know her as you wished,

and you will never see your face in the
faces of your nieces and nephews.

VIII.

Peel the apple with a knife.
Eat the apple without peeling it.

Choose beautiful paper to draw
her head or draw it on a napkin

after dinner. Eat eggs and sausage
and oranges for breakfast

or don't eat. Drink tea or drink
coffee. Call your father to wish him

happy birthday. Use a bandaid when
you scratch your hand on rose thorn, or

bleed freely into your grandmother's
linen. Plant potatoes as you planned.

Let the candles burn down to stumps
or replace them with new ones.

I have wanted to be free to feel,
to welcome you with flowers,

see your smile time after time.
When the apple limb fell, too heavy

with rain and fruit, I painted its wound
with tar. This year I will fertilize

so the tomatoes have no hardship.
I am not afraid to begin to love or

to keep loving. Even in this fire,
it is not fear I feel but heartbreak.

IX.

Because he is afraid and powerful
he lives encircled by water.

We hold her as she dies, turn the chairs
to face each other. We breathe with her

as her child is born, let him
cry in the dark as he mourns her death.

When we don't have what we need,
we use what is nearest. One day he

swims the moat to explore the place
which confuses him. There is food when

he reaches the lit house, and stars
hang from the towering branches

of ancient trees. We must learn to rest
when we are tired. Every morning

the sun rises. Every spring green
returns to the cold climates. Bathe

with her, stand with her in her house
smiling as she shows you the

new wood. If their anger frightens you,
try to understand their grief. If you can't

understand what they say, watch
how they move. It's thunder. She

is young. Tell her the truth. He is near
ninety. Help him cross the street. It's

thunder. Reach for my hand, I will
let you go. It's raining. If you

visit, we will walk down through the fields
and I will show you the river.

The Cocked Finger

I don't know why it is
that the bomb, the end,
seems closer. For years
I've lived with it, *them,*
that incredible dosage
of destruction, and I've sat
in living rooms and discussed living
things, took vacations,
raised my kids as if
the future was what, in spite
of everything, they might enter
like aspirants, not like
lemmings. But now
on our side, as if there were
a side when it comes
to imagining the end of sides,
there's a nice, simple man
and perhaps only a nice man
could press such a button,
believing he was saving
the world for niceness.
And on the other side
there's a terrible dullness
and the dull are always
dangerous, home alone too much
with the latest equipment.
    God, once I cared
if you existed, conjured prayers
just in case.
But it no longer matters—

there's History which is larger
than you, the bully
who knows every pressure
point, every weakness,
eager for the next moment.
I've gotten used to the rapes,
the murders. I eat dinner
and watch them on Channel Six
and nothing shocks me,
not even kindness,
not even, though I'm afraid,
the bomb.
The finger that might
touch it off is cocked
like an apostrophe
on the wrong side of a possessive,
an error so obvious
almost everyone can see it.
          Now here comes
History, pretending
it just wants to be understood.
It's begun to breathe hard,
and there's no record of it
ever being a lover, nor exhausted
from all that it's done.

Bringing Zeus to His Knees

In the drained reflecting pool in the small park
    facing San Francisco City Hall during
      the June 12, 1982 Disarmament Anti-Nuclear Rally
A barechested boy lying on his back, arms behind
    his head, eyes closed,
      sunbasking.
As speaker after speaker gives
    inspiring talk
And the crowd roars and applauds,
    all faces turned toward the stage,
The boy lies there—where last week seagulls floated
    on turquoise ripples.
Does he hear the great pleas for peace?
Or is he dozing?
Perhaps he was listening before
    behind his closed eyes
    his dreamlovegirl or boy appeared
    and glowed and gleamed.
How many loving eyes caress this Vision
    that does not see them?
How many strolling from the rapt crowd
    to rest their ears from the anti-war fervor
    they so much agree with
    and which inspires so many of their poems,
Come upon this Vision and are overcome
    with the dazzling sight of naked boyhood
    armpits and chest and belly and face
    that would bring Zeus to his knees—
I stare uncaring if any see me.
The boy does not open his eyes.

He could be on a hilly grassy meadow
    or inflatable raft in a blue pool
    or on his bed taking a summer nap.
I stare so long so lovingly I'm surprised
    the whole crowd doesn't turn
    to watch me staring and join
    in a staring silent circle
    around this apparition
    fallen from heaven.
The beautiful halfnaked sleeping boy Vision
    says more to me against war,
    against nuclear power, arms race,
    nationalism, imperialism, slavery,
    than all the fiery diatribes put together.
Suddenly I see the boy burn alive,
    his flesh afire writhing screaming pyre,
And the crowd melting flaming agonied forms
    from World War III's imagined holocaust reality,
And then I see him as before
    and see myself kneeling
    by his side
    as before a manger
Lavishing with ecstatic love
    my boylove dream.

Armageddon

I see it in terms of images: humans and angels.
An allegorical war with arms reaching out of clouds
their hands bristling with jagged cut-paper thunderbolts.
On the earth beneath dark women in dark red shawls
cower soliciting mercy, demonstrating their innocent babies.
The Lord, who is a father or the chief executive officer
of a celestial corporation, is displeased.

It will not be like this. I sat in the car one summer
during lunch breaks at the frozen foods plant, reading *Hiroshima*
when it first came out. The picture that is in my mind
is of people, vaporized by an unexpected sun
and only their shadows left burned into the wall behind them.
In their eyes it was the shock of noon forever.

I try to convince myself how that would be:
the lovers in their spacious bedroom with a wall of windows
open gratefully to the air; they are serene and affectionate,
their passion musically resolved; a hand stroking the relaxed dark
     hair.
Then all this struck into nothing, and a flat shadow
like a child's decoration on a funeral dish:
what remains forever to occupy the room.

Leonard Woolf said that there would be war
because the generals, having devised their weapons,
and seen them manufactured, the sleek expensive mechanisms,
would have to try them out, and it is true.
There is no invention of man that has not been used
if it was capable of being used, and these are.
Electric cattle prods defame the soft personal testicles.

But from this Armageddon, at the storm's center,
not even a cry, not even the houses burning.
Less than that, less than anything in the known world.

I asked a young man about twenty, my student, whether
the thought of this possibility was in his mind
and he said yes, even at a loud noise
in the street he would think: now it is happening.
He does not have, as I do, to form images
to imagine the happening: for him it is already there
like the underwear that he puts on in the morning.
It is with him all the time, as his shadow is.

"And he gathered them together into a place called in the
    Hebrew tongue Armageddon.
And the seventh angel poured out his vial into the air;
and there came a great voice out of the temple of heaven,
from the throne, saying, It is done."

The language deceives us, like the language of "peace with
    honor."
If it can be said so nobly, must it not be a noble thing?
So much language hoping to soothe us away from the fact
of death, death without ritual, the procession of ritual mourners
evaporated with him they would have mourned, no distinction.
No context to absorb and make valuable the loss.

The language of the previous verse is better:
"Behold, I come as a thief.
Blessed is he that watcheth, and keepeth his garments,
lest he walk naked, and they see his shame."

There are thieves among us, and they keep their garments.
They accumulate around them garments of steel.
They wait for their final garments of human shadow.

The lovers were naked, the air was calm, the sea
sparkled outside their final window. It was noon
when they became incident.

                            The mushroom cloud
ascending, the clock on the *Bulletin* cover
a minute from midnight. These images
we live under and among. The possibility of absence
so complete we will hardly have known what absence was.

DANIELA GIOSEFFI

from "The Last Fire Feast"

These are the word wounds,
roots of mushroom clouds to rise
from the pockmarked earth:
Guinea, dago, spick,
nigger, polack, wasp, mick,
chink, jap, frog, russkie, red bastard, kike,
bitch, macho pig, gimp, fag, dike —
word wounds to make stench of flesh follow
sprayed dust of children's eyes
melted from wondering sockets, animal skin, thighs,
men's hands, women's sighs
roasted in a final feast of fire
beasts caught like lemmings
in a leap to Armageddon's
false resurrection.
Word wounds rise from visions of charred lips,
burnt books, paper ashes, crumbled libraries, stones
under which plastic pens
and computers are fried amid the last cried
words, smoke to pay lip service—
as Orphic light rages
against the dying of the light
and all dust into dust returns
to the last word, sound,
sigh of a burning leaf turning: "Life live,
leaf live, love life leaf live . . ."

JUDY RAY

Rose Bay Willow Herb

The willow herb, the
rose bay willow herb,
sweeps woods and commons
with pink sunset stripes.
It rises from the black
aftermath of fire
that crackled through thick
undergrowth of trees.
Even after war
it flourishes in
empty lots, in bomb
craters, and like a
phoenix of flora
rises tall and wild,
true fireweed, indeed.
Should the air it spikes,
water it drinks, ash
it grows from become
radioactive,
the invisible
aftermath of a
great folly, perhaps
the willow herb, the
rose bay willow herb,
will still grow wild with
pink sunset stripes and
bloom abundantly.
But who will there be
of our coughing, skin-
flaking, misshapen

kind to perceive a
symbol of hope? And
perhaps the only
phoenix to arise
from that blind folly
will be some tiny
flung molecule of
untainted earth with
no memory of
tall willow herb, wild
rose bay willow herb.

The Garden

We were talking about poetry.
We were talking about nuclear war.
She said she couldn't write about it
because she couldn't imagine it.
I said it was simple. Imagine
this doorknob is the last thing
you will see in this world.
Imagine you happen to be standing
at the door when you look down, about
to grasp the knob, your fingers
curled toward it, the doorknob old
and black with oil from being turned
so often in your hand, cranky
with rust and grease from the kitchen.
Imagine it happens this quickly, before
you have time to think of anything else;
your kids, your own life, what it will mean.
You reach for the knob and the window
flares white, though you see it only
from the corner of your eye because
you're looking at the knob, intent
on opening the back door to the patch
of sunlight on the porch, that garden
spread below the stairs and the single
tomato you might pick for a salad.
But when the flash comes you haven't
thought that far ahead. It is only
the simple desire to move into the sun
that possesses you. The thought
of the garden, that tomato, would have

come after you had taken the knob
in your hand, just beginning to twist it,
and when the window turns white
you are only about to touch it,
preparing to open the door.

JAMES GRABILL

A Dream of the Closeness of Venus

I.

We return to the apartment
in the Colorado mountain town.
The front door swings open.
All the doorknobs, especially
crystal ones, had to be chopped off,
a man tells us, in case
they become irradiated.

I look out the window at Seattle
and see the beginning
of intense light, so quickly
Marilyn and I, with the child
we have with us, climb
under the bed.

II.

It is a large wood-framed bed,
100 years old, or 150.
The dusk is thick, the scent
of fungusy pine needles.
There is a wooden place
under the bed where we can hide,
so we climb in.

We hold one another
and wait for the nuclear blast.

III.

In a few minutes, nothing happens.
A few more, still nothing.

Suddenly, neighbors are crowding
into our room, talking excitedly.

We are on the flat apartment roof,
looking at Seattle, and can see the moon
setting in diamond light
at least ten times
brighter than usual.

IV.

Then a woman notices
a second moon rising
in the south, much larger
than the moon.

As we watch, we see it is Venus,
blue and cratered,
without many swirling clouds,
immensely rising over the town,
almost filling half
of the southern sky,
casting blue light
everywhere around us.

Nobody is afraid.
We look at the blue solar light
on tanks and water purification vats
on other roofs, and blue
down on the streets,

blue melting into the trees
and mountain rock,
as the white moon
sets over the distant ocean,
and Venus nearly
touches Earth
from above us.

v.

It isn't Venus
flying down into the world.
It's Earth
merging with everything around us.

It's Venus bringing the Earth
back to itself,
hovering immensely near us.

⇒✷⇐

Later in the day, I still feel it,
huge in the southern sky.

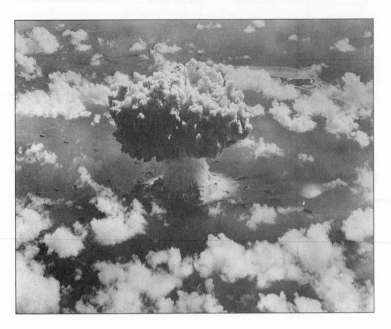

8. Photograph used with permission from Associated Press .

When

I wonder now only when it will happen,
when the young mother will hear the
noise like somebody's pressure cooker
down the block, going off. She'll go out in the yard,
holding her small daughter in her arms,
and there, above the end of the street, in the
air above the line of the trees,
she will see it rising, lifting up
over our horizon, the upper rim of the
gold ball, large as a giant
planet starting to lift up over ours.
She will stand there in the yard holding her daughter,
looking at it rise and glow and blossom and rise,
and the child will open her arms to it,
it will look so beautiful.

W. D. EHRHART

The Way Light Bends

A kind of blindness, that's what's needed now.
Better not to know. Better to notice
the way light bends through trees in winter dusk.

What, after all, does knowledge bring? Cold rage,
the magnitude of history, despair.
A kind of blindness, that's what's needed now

because it's hard enough to pay the bills.
So long as you can still appreciate
the way light bends through trees in winter dusk,

what's possible, what is, what can't be changed
is better left to dreamers, fools and God.
A kind of blindness, that's what's needed now,

the wisdom not to think about what waits
in dark holes beneath the earth. Marvel at
the way light bends through trees in winter dusk

and don't imagine how the light will bend
the way light bends through trees in winter dusk
and burst forever when the missiles fly.
A kind of blindness, that's what's needed now.

The Crab-Apple Crisis

for Martin Bell

*To make this study concrete I have devised a ladder—a metaphorical ladder—
which indicates that there are many continuous paths between a low-level crisis and
an all-out war.* —"On Escalation" by Herman Kahn

Level I: Cold War

Rung 1: Ostensible Crisis
  Is that you, Barnes? Now see here, friend. From
  where I am I can see your boy quite
  clearly soft-shoeing along towards
  my crab-apple tree. And I want you

  to know I can't take that.

Rung 2: Political, Economic and Diplomatic Gestures
                              If you don't
  wipe that smile off your face, I warn you
  I shall turn up the screw of my frog
  transistor above the whirr of your

  lawn-mower.

Rung 3: Solemn and Formal Declarations
                        Now I don't want to sound
  unreasonable but if that boy

  keeps on codding round my apple tree
  I shall have to give serious thought

to taking my belt to him.

Level II: Don't Rock the Boat

Rung 4: Hardening of Positions
                              I thought
you ought to know that I've let the Crows
walk their Dobermann through my stack of
bean canes behind your chrysanthemum

bed.

Rung 5: Show of Force
       You might like a look at how my
boy John handles his catapult. At
nineteen yards he can hit your green-house
pushing four times out of five.

Rung 6: Significant Mobilization
                                        I've asked

the wife to call the boy in for his
coffee, get him to look out a good
supply of small stones.

Rung 7: "Legal" Harassment
                              Sure fire my lawn
spray is soaking your picnic tea-cloth

but I can't be responsible for
how those small drops fall, now can I?

Rung 8: Harassing Acts of Violence

Your
kitten will get a worse clip on her
left ear if she comes any nearer

to my rose-bushes, ma'm.

Rung 9: Dramatic Military Confrontations

Now see here,
sonny, I can see you pretty damn
clearly up here. If you come one step
nearer to that crab-apple tree you'll

get a taste of this strap across your
back.

Level III: Nuclear War Is Unthinkable

Rung 10: Provocative Diplomatic Break

I'm not going to waste my time
gabbing to you any longer, Barnes:
I'm taking this telephone off the

hook.

Rung 11: All Is Ready Status

Margery, bring that new belt of
mine out on the terrace, would you? I
want these crazy coons to see we mean
business.

Rung 12: Large Conventional War

Take that, you lousy kraut. My

pop says you're to leave our crab-apple
tree alone. Ouch! Ow! I'll screw you for
that.

Rung 13: *Large Compound Escalation*
   OK, you've asked for it. The Crows'
dog is coming into your lilac

bushes.

Rung 14: *Declaration of Limited Comventional War*
    Barnes. Can you hear me through this
loud-hailer? OK Well, look. I have
no intention of being the first
to use stones. But I will if you do.

Apart from this I won't let the dog
go beyond your chrysanthemum bed
unless your son actually starts
to climb the tree.

Rung 15: *Barely Nuclear War*
      Why, no. I never

told the boy to throw a stone. It was
an accident, man.

Rung 16: *Nuclear Ultimatum*
      Now see here. Why
have you wheeled your baby into the
tool-shed? We've not thrown stones.

Rung 17: Limited Evacuation

                                      Honey. I

don't want to worry you but their two
girls have gone round to the Joneses'.

Rung 18: Spectacular Show of Force

                                   John.
Throw a big stone over the tree, would
you: but make sure you throw wide.

Rung 19: Justifiable Attack

                                  So we
threw a stone at the boy. Because he
put his foot on the tree. I warned you
now, Barnes.

Rung 20: Peaceful World-Wide Embargo or Blockade
                    Listen, Billy, and you too
Marianne, we've got to teach this cod

a lesson. I'm asking your help in
refusing to take their kids in, or
give them any rights of way, or lend
them any missiles until this is

over.

Level IV: No Nuclear Use

Rung 21: Local Nuclear War
           John. Give him a small fistful
of bricks. Make sure you hit him, but not
enough to hurt.

Rung 22: Declaration of Limited Nuclear War
                        Hello there. Barnes. Now
get this, man. I propose to go on

throwing stones as long as your boy is
anywhere near my tree. Now I can
see you may start throwing stones back and
I want you to know that we'll take that

without going for your wife or your
windows unless you go for ours.

Rung 23: Local Nuclear War—Military
                              We
propose to go on confining our
stone-throwing to your boy beside our

tree: but we're going to let him have
it with all the stones we've got.

Rung 24: Evacuation of Cities—About 70 per cent
                              Sweetie.
Margery. Would you take Peter and
Bernice round to the Switherings?

Things are getting pretty ugly.

Level V: Central Sanctuary

Rung 25: Demonstration Attack on Zone of Interior
                              We'll
start on his cabbage-plot with a strike
of bricks and slates. He'll soon see what we

could do if we really let our hands

slip.

Rung 26: Attack on Military Targets
        You bastards. Sneak in and smash our
crazy paving, would you?

Rung 27: Exemplary Attacks against Property
                                We'll go for
their kitchen windows first. Then put a
brace of slates through the skylight.

Rung 28: Attacks on Population
                                                OK.

Unless they pull out, chuck a stone or
two in the baby's pram in the
shed.

Rung 29: Complete Evacuation—95 per cent
        They've cleared the whole family, eh,
baby and all. Just Barnes and the boy

left. Best get your mom to go round to
the Switherings.

Rung 30: Reciprocal Reprisals
                        Well, if they smash the
bay-window we'll take our spunk out on
the conservatory.

Level VI: Central War

Rung 31: Formal Declaration of General War
Now listen,

Barnes. From now on we're going all
out against you—windows, flowers, the
lot. There's no hauling-off now without
a formal crawling-down.

Rung 32: Slow-Motion Counter-Force War
We're settling

in for a long strong pull, Johnny. We'd
better try and crack their stone stores one
at a time. Pinch the bricks, plaster the
flowers out and smash every last

particle of glass they've got.

Rung 33: Constrained Reduction
We'll have
to crack that boy's throwing-arm with a
paving-stone. Just the arm, mind. I don't
want him killed or maimed for life.

Rung 34: Constrained Disarming Attack
Right, son.

We'll break the boy's legs with a strike of
bricks. If that fails it may have to come
to his head next.

Rung 35: Counter-Force with Avoidance
                        There's nothing else for
it. We'll have to start on the other

two up at the Jones's. If the wife
and the baby gets it, too, it can't
be helped.

Level VII: City Targeting

Rung 36: Counter-City War
                    So it's come to the crunch. His
Maggie against my Margery. The

kids against the kids.

Rung 37: Civilian Devastation
                            We can't afford
holds barred anymore. I'm going all
out with the slates, tools, bricks, the whole damn
shooting-match.

Rung 38: Spasm or Insensate War
                        All right, Barnes. This is it.

Get out the hammer, son: we need our
own walls now. I don't care if the whole
block comes down. I'll get that maniac
if it's the last thing I—Christ. O, Christ.

CHRISTOPHER BUCKLEY

Why I'm in Favor of a Nuclear Freeze

Because we were 18 and still wonderful in our bodies,
because Harry's father owned a ranch and we had
nothing better to do one Saturday, we went hunting
doves among the high oaks and almost wholly quiet air . . .
Traipsing the hills and deer paths for an hour,
we were ready when the first ones swooped—
and we took them down in smoke much like the planes
in the war films of our regimented youth.
                                        Some were dead
and some knocked cold, and because he knew how
and I just couldn't, Harry went to each of them and,
with thumb and forefinger, almost tenderly, squeezed
the last air out of their slight necks.
                                 Our jackets grew
heavy with birds and for a while we sat in the shade
thinking we were someone, talking a bit of girls
who would "go," who wouldn't, how love would probably
always be beyond our reach . . . We even talked of the nuns
who terrified us with God and damnation. We both recalled
that first prize in art, the one pinned to the cork board
in front of class, was a sweet blond girl's drawing
of the fires and coals, the tortured souls of Purgatory.
Harry said he feared eternity until he was 17, and,
if he ever had kids, the last place they would go would be
a parochial school.
                    On our way to the car, having forgotten
which way the safety was off or on, I accidentally discharged
my borrowed 12 gauge, twice actually—one would have been
    Harry's
head if he were behind me, the other my foot, inches to the right.

We were almost back when something moved in the raw, dry
    grass,
and without thinking, and on the first twitch of two tall ears,
we together blew the ever-loving-Jesus out of a jack rabbit
until we couldn't tell fur from dust from blood . . .
                                        Harry has
a family, two children as lovely as any will ever be—
he hasn't hunted in years . . . and that once was enough for me.
Anymore, a good day offers a moment's praise for the lizards
daring the road I run along, or it offers a dusk in which
yellow meadowlarks scrounge fields in the gray autumn light . . .
Harry and I are friends now almost 30 years, and the last time
we had dinner, I thought about that rabbit, not the doves
which we swore we would cook and eat, but that rabbit—
why the hell had we killed it so cold-heartedly? And I saw
that it was simply because we had the guns, because we could.

WILLIAM GREENWAY

The Atom Bum

I think we oughta drop a atom bum own 'em.
—Overheard in a conversation about Nicaragua

Bomb bays open and they kick
him out of yet another door.
Shrieking like a rat he clings until
they step on the fingers stuck from
the amputated fingers of white gloves,
tumbles, burst cigar stub in blubbery
lips, red nose, head-over-down-at-heels
dustpan brogans that can scrape
nickels off a sidewalk, four days
beard, carnation full of coffee
grounds in the lapel of his tuxedo
coat, one hand holding his bowler on,
the other to an umbrella with red
bandana bundle in the crook
opening to let him float down
through blue air over khaki
jungle, swaying to snag
suspenders on the spire of the
adobe cathedral above the cobbled
square, its own bums asleep
in banana leaves.
He hangs all day above the land
whose poor and rich walk in to lay
automatic weapons down, look up
at him and weep, kneel and embrace.
Soon he dies of burns, and his bones
glow through the night like a star.

Terminal Colloquy

O where will you go when the blinding flash
Scatters the seed of a million suns?
And what will you do in the rain of ash?

I'll draw the blinds and pull down the sash,
And hide from the light of so many noons.
But how will it be when the blinding flash

Disturbs your body's close-knit mesh,
Bringing to light your lovely bones?
What will you wear in the rain of ash?

I will go bare without my flesh,
My vertebrae will click like stones.
Ah. But where will you dance when the blinding flash

Settles the city in a holy hush?
I will dance alone among the ruins.
Ah. And what will you say to the rain of ash?

I will be charming. My subtle speech
Will weave close turns and counter turns—
No. What will you say to the rain of ash?
Nothing, after the blinding flash.

Nuclear Winter

After the first terror
      people
Were more helpful to each other—
As in a blizzard
Much comradeliness, help, even
                    laughter:
The pride of getting through tough times.

Even, months later,
When the snow fell in June,
We felt a kind of pride in
             our
"Unusual weather"
And joked about the wild geese
Migrating south,
Quacking over the 4th of July presidential honkings.
It was, people said,
The way it had been in the Old Days . . .

Until the hunger of the next year.
Then we came to our senses
And began to kill each other.

NICHOLAS SAMARAS

Nuclear Winter

This far I know: We will all singularly choose where to lie down,
stoke the night, read Darwin, Writings of the Desert Saints. Those
with tattered dissertations may migrate to New York City, ar-
guing our occlusion. They will peer as through tinted glasses, un-
pack hasty papers, briefs, workable stopwatches, ampules of
cologne. Their hands will smell fragrant. Soon I will move to the
furthest part of myself. I will shore up the framehouse in the
foothills of Wyoming, wedged between a rusted mesa, a railway
trailing itself like February breath. I have weighed my days
against the distance on the horizon I think my sight may carry
me. I plan this, the temperature of our lives forcing the choice. I
will lie down in my father's bed, open windows and let glassy
winds bleach me like the femurs and spoked teeth of sagebrush.
Far off, the sounds of frenzy in the dark hills. Echoes of violence
and dull explosions. Pocks of fires against the nights. Cries of hun-
ger ebbing. The long, brittle ache in my bones. Outside, I'll feel
the earth cool, blur and deepen, watch muledeer and hinterland
wolves approach warily for warmth. Together, we'll huddle in
the garden, face to fur, embracing what is human, what is ani-
mal, look up to the light unraveling, the sky's cataract.

PETER BLUE CLOUD (ARONIAWENRATE)

Deeper Than a Dream

(for oboe)

like a memory beyond death
I awake to find myself become
a mass of obsidian far underground,
having witnessed light only once
and briefly, I retain that light
at the core of my being,
                              brighter
than any remembered sun.
    A thought intruded:
"Can a mass of obsidian
have being?" And the
thought caused a fracture
which shook the western
edge of a continent.
    Now, when I surface,
an earthworm will worry
a tunnel thru the fracture
and thus will begin
my disintegration,
                          I thought,
settling down to
further centuries.

TERRANCE KEENAN

After the Neutron

I like to think the first one
will not be a looter
since the private things
of a hundred towns
will be so much the same.
No, someone would get to our place
a long time after, someone curious,
a scientist,
someone with enough memory
when finding the front door locked
to go round to the back.

In the mudroom,
with its old beige walls,
he would see the jumble of boots and coats
that are there winter or summer,
with the several odd things
we never found a place for.
The kitchen will look like
we had just finished breakfast
because I am sure it will happen in the morning.

He won't breathe the air we did
but wisely carry his own.
After a tour he may notice the kitchen
the most lived-in room
and our minor flare for colorful clutter.
But he'll be quickly drawn
to the larger houses up the street
and the empty red stone church
crisp against the birdless sky.

They're Family Men

I say to myself, they're
family men, have children, some
grandchildren. And though they haven't
held their wives as they pushed,
veins strained like April rivers
or carried the newborn while its hairs
held the wet pattern of its birth, still
they must have stood in woolen bathrobes heating bottles
must have rocked the squalling child till it sucked
    and softened into ovaled arms.
Or if not that, they must have once
touched their finger to a cheek, pink
as silkwood blossom, head pussy willow soft,
or seen a mouth open in first smiles,
the tiny point of the gums, the half-a-moon grin,
and the sounds—
they couldn't help hearing the sounds,
the roll of the r's, the gurgle in the bath.

They love their children.
They see they don't have diaper rash,
wear shoes too small or play in the street.
They fasten headlights to their bicycles
and coax them to eat carrots.

Yet they work for Bechtel. They work for Lockheed.
They work at the nuclear power plants at
Hanford, Washington; West Valley, New York.
They dump wastes in the San Francisco Bay.
And they say, "Don't worry."

They say, "It's safe."
They say, "The economy, jobs, and fuel."
And I ask myself, how?
I ask myself how? and what do they
tell themselves?

When they dance at their daughters' wedding,
when they dance at their sons' wedding,
when they drink imported champagne and roast beef is
excellent, little ones in party clothes
crawl under linen tablecloths
and even the grandmother two-steps a bit in blue shoes—
at night when they get into bed and kiss their happy wives good-
                                                    night,
how? how do they keep from thinking
that their grandchildren will never see grandchildren?

ALLAN COOPER

To an Unborn Child

Strategy maps are placed neatly on long tables.

   The man in the uniform pores over them endlessly, think-
ing strike, counter-strike. A spider the size of the dot New York
descends, unravelling from the ceiling lamp, lands on a sheet.
The general leans forward, flicks it away.

   In the movement of one finger the death of millions.

I think of old spruce in the bog up the road,
all life gone from them,
old man's beard and lichen
the only things
that speak of anything living . . .

I could mull there for days
until the only idea I have left
is as small and compact
as one seed shed from a cone, sprouting now
in old snow water.

A Lear jet leaves its white plume
in the sky. I remember a day at Caribou Plains
when fifteen jets went over, one after the other,
silencing the drone
of bees, low wind through marsh grass.

I thought then
that maybe this is the end,
maybe the first bomb will fall any minute now
leaving me speechless, aglow,
the death-terror permanently etched on my face . . .

But after a while
even the white plumes dissolved,
and the wind sound came back, a ptarmigan
flew up, its heavy flutter echoed off the backwall
of trees.

I have learned patient lessons
from insects—
the spider under his leaf,
waiting for the life-rhythms from the web;
the ant, still on a stone,
waiting for the advancing army to come;
the killer bee, cruising around the hive,
waiting for the infra-red picture
of a warm body
to come into view . . .

And I have learned terrible lessons
from children,
playing war games on a video screen,
the death star
reaching out
for total annihilation . . .

Perhaps death
is the final exhilaration,
or perhaps we have grown too comfortable

in our duplicate homes,
the unexpected
drawing us in
like filings
around a magnetic core.

❧

Basho said:

Spider, if you had a voice,
what would you sing,
swaying in fall wind?

And I say,

Spider, if you had a voice,
what would you say
as the light dims in the brain,

aggression boils like black water
from a broken water main,
no one can stop it,

as the moon darkens in the still of the month
and tracks of spacemen
disappear

in the wind
of a lunar
storm.

❧

I speak to an unborn child.
If I could tell you one thing of meaning

it would be to love everything, to love people,
even though it's hard sometimes,
to love the lesson of the unfolding leaf,
to laugh, for it is only a child who can laugh
in utter abandon, for the joy of it,
the joy of a cat leaping at a blown grassblade,
the cricket adrift on a woodchip boat,
the joy of your own reflection in a puddle,
at one with clouds . . .

❧

And finally there is only one reason to save this life.
If we could look through a microscope,
now, we could see
cells dividing,
random growth
that will amount to
one leaf
aglow at dusk, on a tree in a garden,
whose only purpose
is to transform
the light.

PAUL ZIMMER

Because of Duties, Zimmer Had Forgotten the Forest

Now I see the moon rise like primitive memory
And think of solitary times, how crickets etch
Themselves into an evening like this. I watch
The humbling process of darkness begin in trees,
Their great canopies begin to grow the stars.
I do not wish to dwell upon this splendor;
I build fire and back their glister away with my glare.

I gaze at flames and recall the ferocity of bombs,
Distant towers in dawn light, the countdown until
There are no more numbers, then the flash
And deadly roll of the shock wave,
Blinded animals calling, shacks and bushes burning.

I have no comfort until new light softens my fire
And dawn begins to piece itself through leaves.
Then I recall that burning wood is delicate kinship,
That no matter what we do to trees they love
Us to the end, stroking our bones with root tips,
Toppling the markers to purify graves.

from "An American Peace"

In this third year of Reagan, my 27th year,
I dreamed we walked the warehouses
of the lower North Side, down to the Ohio

where we stripped. In a purple mist,
through shimmery water, we stroked out,
borne up by small waves,

and at midstream I faced Pittsburgh,
three bridges at my back, to one side
Stephanie, to the other my first son,

only our heads above water, bobbing
and bobbing, when in front of us he surfaced,
Jacob, our youngest, and it seemed

that from his head, his large infant head,
the skyline loomed, the sun upsprung behind
like a brilliant furnace;

tower and office and condominium
blazed red, radiant, forming a crown
of sorts, a wild wig of city,

so that we laughed.
Then the sky flashed white
as if the sun had dropped closer:
one second, two seconds, three seconds,
blast: deafness, ringing, Jacob's screaming . . .
I reached, saw my hands, saw the bones of my hands

and saw Jacob dig at his eyes, screaming . . .
which I couldn't stop or relieve, but I grabbed him
thinking *water*, dunked him
and held him hard.
                              I turned to the cloud
mushrooming, the light in pinks and blues,
all the while wrestling Jacob, whom I no longer hear.
A whooshing sound started, heat-wind in a wave,
and I was driven under, accelerated through black waters,
giddy with fear until I loosened my grip,
relaxed my shoulders, my neck,
and my whole body lightened, rarefied,
the blackness through me and with me and in me,
when my mind like a dim flashlight
began to sweep in search of something—
something recognizable—
but there was nothing, only water,
and the mind aware of itself.

Tale Before the End of the World

We never had any doubt the world would end.
The message wavered over the air waves
in a bodiless echo. Sam packed the car
with peaches, wine, some macadamias we'd saved.
No need for a map of the mundane, or of the stars
that hid themselves in shame for us.
The children watched our faces closely,
hugging their dolls to their breasts.

Up we wound, higher and higher into ponderosas
clinging to the rain-scrubbed mountains.
A hawk swirled and floated over the road,
oblivious to the early chill, the emptiness
broadcast from the city's heart below.
Who would have thought such a world
could end, suddenly, like a dream?
We turned away from the thought.

Sorrow rose from the bark, from a string
of ants laboring under their tiny loads.
Sorrow balanced on a branch and sang
its sparrow song, and wrung its squirrel hands.
Sorrow opened and closed the breeze's lips,
sorrow seethed in sap, in leaf-vein, in blood.
The sorrow caught the fingertips of Anne,
our child, pulling her up from the ground.

I won't let the world die, she cried out
as the sorrow multiplied her soul and she
swelled until she loomed huge as a thunderhead—

her hands churning their windmills,
her eyes beaming their floodlights in farewell.
A human tornado, a magnet, she drew out
the poison from the world's silos,
from the minds and mouths of terror.

And that's how she saved the world.
We repacked the car and drove home,
though Anne never returned to us at all.
I spoon out the darkness and the light
at dinner time, and later touch my son
unborn beneath my skin, and hold my husband
in his death-tormented sleep. I lie in bed,
stricken by the silence of the house.

Silence at the End of the World

Beads of ice hang from the coral tree
and still there is no rain.
The sky does not open.
Not here. Not yet.
We are in peril.
Men are setting fire to the earth.

Silence sits on the words,
lies across my heart until I cannot breathe.
Do we ever get used to this fear?
I come to you hoping to burn,
to melt the boundaries between *you* and *I*
as if our bodies could disappear, one into the other.

In my dream the woman refuses to put down her gun.
A bullet in the brain, she says.
It is the only solution:
Our minds have become instruments of torture.
Our bodies no longer reflect heat nor light.
Our dead will not rise from the earth singing.

The man in the desert cradles his head in his hands
wailing like a lost child: fuck you, fuck you God.
He has found his mantra.
He is the man with the axe
splitting open his own head.
He could be my father, my brother.

Ravens fly over the house,
huddle in the branches of the coral tree

cracking the ice with their beaks.
Their cries like arrows pierce the air:
How far to the waters of the rivermouth,
the sacred burial grounds, the holy circle of stones?

My love, tell me it is not too late:
that when the sky breaks open it will be with rain,
that the drought of words will create breath again,
that our voices will shatter the silence at the end of the world.

DAVID ROMTVEDT

Eating Dinner at My Sister's

It's another warm night.
The grass is growing.
The city shouts its city song.
The birds and bugs clack
and buzz, saying, "Here we are!"
How small the yard is
and how close the house
next door. House after house.

In the middle of our dinner
the atomic bomb falls.
For a moment I feel terror,
then, having waited so long,
this terror turns to relief.
I set down my dinner
and watch. Then I run
screaming in the yard.
Blinded, I collide with my sister
who takes my hand.

This close, what is left
of a person is shadow,
pale gray on a shattered wall
or dark on the dusty earth.

The rising mushroom spirals toward us.
My sister opens her mouth and swallows.
The moon rises and its cold light seems warm.

I slow my breathing to count the breaths:
one—do not flee adversity,
two—only good can come of facing fear,
three—a single pure soul
can save the earth.

I thank my sister for swallowing
our bomb and wonder how many
have done it before, how many
whose names I cannot say.

GATHERED AT THE RIVER

9. Photograph used with permission from Los Alamos National Laboratory.

High Noon at Los Alamos

To turn a stone
with its white squirming
underneath, to pry the disc
from the sun's eclipse—white heat
coiling in the blinded eye: to these malign
necessities we come
from the dim time of dinosaurs
who crawled like breathing lava
from the earth's cracked crust, and swung
their tiny heads above the lumbering tons
of flesh, no bigger than a fist
clenched to resist the white flash
in the sky the day the sun-flares
pared them down to relics for museums,
turned glaciers back, seared Sinai's
meadows black—the ferns withered, the swamps
were melted down to molten mud, the cells
uncoupled, recombined, and madly
multiplied, huge trees toppled to the ground,
the slow life there abandoned hope,
a caterpillar stiffened in the grass.
Two apes, caught in the act of coupling,
made a mutant child
who woke to sunlight wondering, his mother
torn by the huge new head
that forced the narrow birth canal.

As if compelled to repetition
and to unearth again
white fire at the heart of matter—fire

we sought and fire we spoke,
our thoughts, however elegant, were fire
from first to last—like sentries set to watch
at Argos for the signal fire
passed peak to peak from Troy
to Nagasaki, triumphant echo of the burning
city walls and prologue to the murders
yet to come—we scan the sky
for that bright flash,
our eyes stared white from watching
for the signal fire that ends
the epic—a cursèd line
with its caesura, a pause
to signal peace, or a rehearsal
for the silence.

BARBARA LA MORTICELLA

A Liturgy for Trinity

I.

Our fathers of the atomic industry
thought there was a chance
New Mexico might be destroyed
when they exploded Trinity,

or even that the entire earth
would flash. They took the chance:

stationed soldiers in bunkers and foxholes
close to the blast to see . . .

"I was driving my sister home, and we were
about 20 miles away, when she looked out the
window and shouted, 'What's that light?' The thing
is, my sister is blind . . ."

Oh immense light boiling out of the ground:
iridescent colors—red, purple, orange:
pistons and wheels like ten suns moving across the sky.

"We were in this big desert when the bomb went off,
and suddenly the desert looked tiny and the mountains looked
tiny. I've never seen things the same since."

Petals of light falling on the backs of the
animals in the fields,
spokes of light spinning in the genes of the unborn,
saucers of light landing on the platelets of the blood,
coins of light across the eyes of the now dead.

꧁

Our mute mother of this atomic age,
we need to see things never the same again also.

Never again only two eyes with their left and their right
separated as soon as they're named.

Never again, please, this third eye with its blindness:
this eye of the Trinity waving a green goodbye.

There needs to be more than a fourth eye that shrinks like a
violet from the light of the blaze.

For even five eyes aren't enough to help us see over the top
of this huge pile of bodies—

so we've opened the sixth eye of smoke
and the seventh of darkness.

II.

Seeking perfect security, the world in 1980
spent a million dollars a minute on defense.

The fathers turn away from each other, but are
joined at the waist by the hinge of their darkness.

In the last days of the Piscean age,
perfect materialism snorts uranium like cocaine;
perfect spiritualism builds a nuclear submarine called
Corpus Christi, watches the seas boil.

Without telling them,
Russia used the people of the Urals like mops
to wipe up a nuclear accident.

When today's army talks about integrated battlefield,
it means a field where the soldiers are nuked & gassed & shot
all at once. Still, the Ayatollah said death is preferable
to an imperfect world.

In the last days of the Piscean age,
CIA agents passed out LSD on Haight St.

The President ordered opium stockpiled outside the cities
for after the blast.

No matter what happens,
Corpus Christi is secure—

The rights of the bodies of Christ
to form a huge pile reaching all the way into the sky.

III.

Light a candle for Thomas O'Dell
Portland lawyer who died of leukemia at 45
20 years after he was a soldier
at Yucca flats.

He didn't ask to have x-ray vision,
but after he'd stood with his back to the blast,
shielding his eyes as he'd been told,
and saw—clearly—his hands with the blood in them,
and the bones white, cuneiform, startling—

he was never the same again. Some unknown
line of defense breached. All the mute bones
articulate:

his hands like mountains trembling in the sky,
his hands a puzzle heaped on his wife's thigh,
his hands two piles of coins.

><

Sometimes when it's nearing dusk
there's a sheen on old boards
and on the surface of the dark soil

as if the sky had come to nestle in things,
meeting them on their own terms for a change,
with a blue that's neither melancholy nor cold.

In the course of this kiss, this delicate exchange
the light is ineluctably drawn into the cut grain of things
and the darkness has stars folded up into it
like blossoms of light. . . .

EDWARD A. DOUGHERTY

Why I Think About Hiroshima and Nagasaki

I'm happy. I've got
plenty to eat.

Pumpkins cooked
in their shells; potatoes baked
under the hot ground.

       I wasn't alive, so I
       don't remember. 1945.
       War.

He took a woman by the hands
but her skin . . .

       Look at these hands,
       they have plenty of fingers.

her skin slipped off
in huge, glovelike pieces.

       I'm happy. My life is good.
       Tony Medwid showed me
       a roofing tile from an old
       Catholic cathedral
       ruined by the atomic bomb.

Another woman huddled herself
around her child—dead
for four days.

The clay had bubbled in the heat.

She held that baby
even after the body
had begun to decay.

"Imagine," he said,
"what would happen
to the human body."

ANDREA COLLINS

Hiroshima Day at the Riviera Coffeeshop

No counterman expects stumps
colored yellow sunrise
to appear aimed at him
like gunbarrels. Watch him try
to hand the woman hot coffee:
stir the air where the hands should be.
Her wrists nudge his fingers.
Abstract

the tips of long pink nails
caressing a lover, abstract
the choice to punch back when attacked.

She waits at the counter
for the mug to cool; her stumps
are the sensitive palms
of her hands. You can read them.
Perhaps

she put up her hands to cover her face
as she was blown off tiptoe
by the sun she thought she saw
out the classroom window
her first Hiroshima Day.

"My hands are bags of water,"
she thinks. "Water. Teacher,
take me to the river
to soothe my hands" that burst

and the skin hung, rags
flapping at her wrists.

Peripheral nerves come back.
Perhaps at home she drinks hot coffee,
fingerless hot mitts protecting her stumps.
Perhaps she straps on the big metal hands,
bigger than the small pairs doled out by the hundreds
after the surrender. She can do
anything with her teleologic beauties:

on the table next to the bed,
the large, austere hooks.
She can turn the pages
of books, lift a hot cup
to her lips, masturbate
with metal forefingers and thumbs
spread by a strap system
passing over her back, worked
by the hunching of her shoulders.
Notice: the woman knows how
to tremble, not the hands.

Welcome to Hiroshima

is what you first see, stepping off the train:
a billboard brought to you in living English
by Toshiba Electric. While a channel
silent in the TV of the brain

projects those flickering re-runs of a cloud
that brims its risen columnful like beer
and, spilling over, hangs its foamy head,
you feel a thirst for history: what year

it started to be safe to breathe the air,
and when to drink the blood and scum afloat
on the Ohta River. But no, the water's clear,
they pour it for your morning cup of tea

in one of the countless sunny coffee shops
whose plastic dioramas advertise
mutations of cuisine behind the glass:
a pancake sandwich; a pizza someone tops

with a maraschino cherry. Passing by
the Peace Park's floral hypocenter (where
how bravely, or with what mistaken cheer,
humanity erased its own erasure),

you enter the memorial museum
and through more glass are served, as on a dish
of blistered grass, three mannequins. Like gloves
a mother clips to coatsleeves, strings of flesh

hang from their fingertips; or as if tied
to recall a duty for us, *Reverence*
the dead whose mourners too shall soon be dead,
but all commemoration's swallowed up

in questions of bad taste, how re-created
horror mocks the grim original,
and thinking at last *They should have left it all*
you stop. This is the wristwatch of a child.

Jammed on the moment's impact, resolute
to communicate some message, although mute,
it gestures with its hands at eight-fifteen
and eight-fifteen and eight-fifteen again,

while tables of statistics on the wall
update the news by calling on a roll
of tape, death gummed on death, and in the case
adjacent, an exhibit under glass

is glass itself: a shard the bomb slammed in
a woman's arm at eight-fifteen, but some
three decades on—as if to make it plain
hope's only as renewable as pain,

and as if all the unsung
debasements of the past may one day come
rising to the surface once again—
worked its filthy way out like a tongue.

GALWAY KINNELL

The Fundamental Project of Technology

A flash! A white flash sparkled!
—Tatsuichiro Akizuki
   from *Concentric Circles of Death*

Under glass, glass dishes which changed
in color; pieces of transformed beer bottle;
a household iron; bundles of wire become solid
lumps of iron; a pair of pliers; a ring of skull-
bone fused to the inside of a helmet; a pair of eyeglasses
taken off the eyes of a witness, without glass,
which vanished, when a white flash sparkled.

An old man, possibly a soldier back then,
now reduced down to one who soon will die,
sucks at the cigaret dangling from his lip, peers
at the uniform, scorched, of some tiniest schoolboy,
sighs out bluish mists of his own ashes over
a pressed tin lunch box well crushed back then when
the word *future* first learned, in a white flash, to jerk tears.

On the bridge outside, in navy black, a group
of schoolchildren line up, hold it, grin at a flash-pop,
swoop in a flock across grass, see a stranger, cry,
hello! hello! hello! and soon, *goodbye! goodbye!*
having pecked up the greetings that fell half unspoken
and the going-sayings that those who went the day
it happened a white flash sparkled did not get to say.

If all a city's faces were to shrink back all at once
from their skulls, would a new sound come into existence,
audible above moans eaves extracts from wind that smoothes
the grass on graves; or raspings heart's-blood greases still;
or wails babies trill born already skillful at the grandpa's rattle;
or infra-screams bitter-knowledge's speechlessness
memorized, at that white flash, inside closed-forever mouths?

To de-animalize human mentality, to purge it of obsolete
evolutionary characteristics, in particular of death,
which foreknowledge terrorizes the contents of skulls with,
is the fundamental project of technology; however,
the mechanisms of *pseudologica fantastica* require
if you would establish deathlessness you must first eliminate
those who die; a task attempted, when a white flash sparkled.

Unlike the trees of home, which continually evaporate
along the skyline, the trees here have been enticed down
toward world-eternity. No one knows which gods they enshrine.
Does it matter? Awareness of ignorance is as devout
as knowledge of knowledge. Or more so. Even though not know-
    ing,
sometimes we weep, from surplus gratitude, even though know-
    ing,
twice already on earth sparkled a flash, a white flash.

The children go away. By nature they do. And by memory,
in scorched uniforms, holding tiny crushed lunch tins.
All the ecstacy-groans of each night call them back, satori
their ghostliness back into the ashes, in the momentary shrines,
the thankfulness of arms, from which they will go
again and again, until the day flashes and no one lives
to look back and say, a flash, a white flash sparkled.

Return to Hiroshima

1. *Bombardier*

Coming out of the station he expected
To bump into the cripple who had clomped,
Bright pencils trailing, across his dreams

For fifteen years. Before setting out
He was ready to offer both his legs,
His arms, his sleepless eyes. But it seemed

There was no need: it looked a healthy town,
The people gay, the new streets dancing
In the famous light. Even the War Museum

With its photos of the blast, the well-mapped
Rubble, the strips of blackened skin,
Moved one momentarily. After all,

From the window one could watch picnickers
Plying chopsticks as before, the children
Bombing carp with rice-balls. Finding not

What he had feared, he went home cured at last.
Yet minutes after getting back in bed
A wood leg started clomping, a thousand

Eyes leapt wild, and once again he hurtled
Down a road paved white with flesh. On waking
He knew he had gone too late to the wrong

Town, and that until his own legs numbed
And eyes went dim with age, somewhere
A fire would burn that no slow tears could quench.

ii. *Pilot*

All right, let them play with it,
Let them feel all hot and righteous,
Permit them the savage joy of

Deploring my inhumanity,
And above all let them bury
Those hundred thousands once again:

I too have counted the corpses,

And say this: if Captain X
Has been martyred by the poets,
Does that mean I have to weep

Over his "moments of madness"?
If he dropped the bomb, and he did,
If I should sympathize, and I do

(I too have counted the corpses),

Has anyone created a plaint
For those who shot from that red sun
Of Nineteen Forty-One? Or

Tried to rouse just one of those
Thousand Jonahs sprawled across
the iron-whale bed of Saipan Bay?

I too have counted the corpses.

And you, Tom Staines, who got it
Huddled in "Sweet Lucy" at my side,
I still count yours, regretting

You did not last to taste the
Exultation of learning that
"Perhaps nine out of ten of us"

(I too have counted the corpses)

Would not end up as fertilizer
For next spring's rice crop. I'm no
Schoolboy, but give me a pencil

And a battlefield, and I'll make you
A formula: take one away
From one, and you've got bloody nothing.

I too have counted the corpses.

III. *Survivors*

Of the survivors there was only one
That spoke, but he spoke as if whatever
Life there was hung on his telling all.

And he told all. Of the three who stayed,
Hands gripped like children in a ring, eyes
floating in the space his wall had filled,

Of the three who stayed on till the end,
One leapt from the only rooftop that
Remained, the second stands gibbering

At a phantom wall, and it's feared the last,
The writer who had taken notes, will
Never write another word. He told all.

KURIHARA SADAKO

When We Say "Hiroshima"

When we say "Hiroshima,"
do people answer, gently,
"Ah, Hiroshima?"
Say "Hiroshima," and hear "Pearl Harbor."
Say "Hiroshima," and hear "Rape of Nanjing."
Say "Hiroshima," and hear of women and children
thrown into trenches, doused with gasoline,
and burned alive in Manila.
Say "Hiroshima,"
and hear echoes of blood and fire.

Say "Hiroshima,"
and we don't hear, gently,
"Ah, Hiroshima."
As one, the dead and the voiceless masses of Asia
spit out the anger
of all those we made victims.
That we may say "Hiroshima,"
and hear in reply, gently,
"Ah, Hiroshima,"
we must lay down in fact
the arms we were supposed to lay down.
We must get rid of all foreign bases of foreign nations.
Until that day Hiroshima will be
a city of ruthlessness and bitter distrust.
We will be pariahs
scorched by remnant radioactivity.

That we may say "Hiroshima,"
and hear in reply, gently,
"Ah, Hiroshima,"
we must
cleanse
our filthy hands.

translated from the Japanese by Richard H. Minear

CAROLYN FORCHÉ

The Garden Shukkei-en

By way of a vanished bridge we cross this river
As a cloud of lifted snow would ascend a mountain.

She has always been afraid to come here.

It is the river she most
Remembers, the living
And the dead both crying for help

A world that allowed neither tears nor lamentation

The matsu trees brush her hair as she passes
Beneath them, as do the shining strands of barbed wire

Where this lake is, there was a lake,
Where these black pine grow, there grew black pine.

Where there is no teahouse I see a wooden teahouse
and the corpses of those who slept in it.

On the opposite bank of the Ota, a weeping willow
Etches its memory of their faces into the water

Where light touches the face, the character for heart is written.

She strokes a burnt trunk wrapped in straw:
I was weak and my skin hung from my fingertips like cloth

Do you think for a moment we were human beings to them?

She comes to the stone angel holding paper cranes
Not an angel, but a woman where she once had been

Who walks through the garden Shukkei-en
Calling the carp to the surface by clapping her hands

Do Americans think of us?

So she began as we squatted over the toilets
If you want, I'll tell you, but nothing I say will be enough

We tried to dress our burns with vegetable oil
Her hair is the white froth of rice rising up kettlesides, her mind
    also
In the post-war years she thought deeply about how to live

The common greeting *dozo-yoroshiku* is please take care of me
All *hibakusha* still alive were children then

A cemetery seen from the air is a child's city

I don't like this particular red flower because
It reminds me of a woman's brain crushed under a roof

Perhaps my language is too precise, and therefore difficult to
    understand?

We have not, all these years, felt what you call happiness
But at times, with good fortune, we experience something close

As our life resembles life, and this garden the garden
And in the silence surrounding what happened to us

It is the bell to awaken God that we've heard ringing

MAXINE KUMIN

How to Survive Nuclear War

after reading Ibuse's *Black Rain*

Brought low in Kyoto
too sick with chills and fever
to take the bullet train to Hiroshima
I am jolted out of this geography
pursued by Nazis, kidnapped, stranded
when the dam bursts, my life
always in someone else's hands.
Room service brings me tea and aspirin.

This week the Holy Radish
Festival. Pure white daikons
one foot long grace all the city's shrines.
Earlier a celebration for the souls
of insects farmers may have trampled on
while bringing in the harvest.
Now shall I repent?
I kill to keep whatever
pleases me. Last summer
to save the raspberries
I immolated hundreds of coppery
Japanese beetles.

In some respects
Ibuse tells me
radiation sickness is less
terrible than cancer. The hair
comes out in patches. Teeth
break off like matchsticks

at the gumline but the loss
is painless. Burned skin itches,
peels away in strips.
Everywhere the black rain fell
it stained the flesh like a tattoo.
Weeks later when survivors must expel
day by day in little pisses
the membrane lining their bladders
pain becomes an extreme grammar.

I understand we did this.
I understand
we may do this again
before it is done to us.
In case it is thought of
to do to us.

Just now the homage that
I could not pay the irradiated dead
gives rise to a dream.
In it, a festival to mourn
the ritual maiming of the ginkgo,
pollarding that lops all natural growth
from the tumorous stump
years of pruning creates. I note
that these faggots are burned.
I observe that the smoke
is swallowed with great ceremony.
Thereupon I see
that every severed shoot comes back,
takes on a human form,
fan-shaped, ancient, all-knowing,
tattered like us.

This means
we are all to be rescued.

Though we eat animals
and wear their skins,
though we crack mountains
and insert rockets in them

this signifies
we will burn and go up.
We will be burned and come back.

I wake naked, parched,
my skin striped by sunlight.
Under my window
a line of old ginkgos hunkers down.
The new sprouts that break from
their armless shoulders are
the enemies of despair.

Shadow

Vaporized—
with no trace.
Relieved of anything
perceptible to bury
or cremate: a broken
cistern of photons,
waves like grain
moving.

The monument:
a gray stain fused
in concrete, a shadow
cast on three steps in Nagasaki
for a moment, by the silvery flash
of the explosion;
etched there by light
from the suns
that exposed it. Not a man.

Not a woman. An effigy: human
by deduction,
like a cloak.

I try to touch
a dark blotch on the screen
the commentators' talk
flows over. Feeling
my mind refuse
invasion, re-fuse
stain, stiffen against

shadowy webs
of the world and its end;

abiding them
in the silo of my body
—there is no other place—
until they are born,
gray, and can dismantle
the silos, shining
by their thousands
on the earth.

Radiation

A LITURGY FOR AUGUST 6 AND 9

A Call to Worship

Stand in the sun long enough to remember

that nothing is made without light
spoken so firmly
our flesh is its imprint.

Whirlpool nebula, the eye of the cat, snow
crystals, knotholes, the x-ray diffraction
pattern of beryl—all these echo the original

word that hums in the uncharted mind.
Listen and answer.

Responses

If the corn shrinks into radiant air and our bread
is a burning cinder
                              like chaff we will wither and burn

If the thrush and oriole vanish, borne off into the wind,
unhoused and barren
                              we forget how to sing and mourn

If our cities and mountains fall into the fields
and sleep with the stones

how can we leaf through old photographs and letters
how summon our lives
                              our hands will be smoke

Confession ·

The bomb exploded in the air above the city destroyed hospitals
markets houses temples burned thousands in darkened air in
radiant air hid them in rubble one hundred thousand dead. As
many lived were crippled diseased they bled from inside from the
mouth from sores in the skin they examined their children daily
for signs scars invisible one day might float to the surface of the
body the next red and poisoned risen from nowhere

We made the scars and the radiant air.
We made people invisible as numbers.
We did this.

An Ancient Text

There is a dim glimmering of light
unput out in men. Let them walk
that the darkness overtake them not.

Private Meditation

(Shore birds over
the waves dipping and turning their wings together,
their leader invisible, her signal their

common instinct, the long work of years
felt in a moment's flash and veer—

we could be like that.)

Common Prayer

And when we have had enough profit and loss
enough asbestos, coal dust, enough slick
oil and dead fish on the coast; enough
of the chatter and whine and bite
of stale laws and the burn
of invisible ions

then we are ready to notice
light in the gauze of the red dragonfly's wing
and in the spider's web at dusk; ready to walk
through the fallen yellow leaves, renaming
birds and animals.

We will not forget our dead.
We sharpen the scythe until it sings loud
our one original name.

10. Photograph used with permission from UPI/Bettmann.

DENISE LEVERTOV

Gathered at the River

for Beatrice Hawley and John Jagel

As if the trees were not indifferent . . .

A breeze flutters the candles but the trees give off
a sense of listening, of hush.

The dust of August on their leaves.
But it grows dark. Their dark green
is something known about, not seen.

But summer twilight takes away
only color, not form. The tree-forms,
massive trunks and the great domed heads,
leaning in towards us, are visible,

a half-circle of attention.

They listen because the war
we speak of, the human war with ourselves,

the war against earth,
against nature,
is a war against them.

The words are spoken
of those who survived a while,
living shadowgraphs, eyes fixed forever

on witnessed horror,
who survived to give
testimony, that no-one
may plead ignorance.
Contra naturam. The trees,
the trees are not indifferent.

We intone together, *Never again,*

we stand in a circle,
singing, speaking, making vows,

remembering the dead
of Hiroshima,
of Nagasaki.
We are holding candles: we kneel to set them
afloat on the dark river
as they do
there in Hiroshima. We are invoking

saints and prophets,
heroes and heroines of justice and peace,
to be with us, to help us
stop the torment of our evil dreams . . .

Windthreatened flames bob on the current . . .

They don't get far from shore. But none capsizes
even in the swell of a boat's wake.

The waxy paper cups sheltering them
catch fire. But still the candles
sail their gold downstream.

And still the trees ponder our strange doings, as if
well aware that if we fail,
we fail also for them:
if our resolves and prayers are weak and fail

there will be nothing left of their slow and innocent wisdom,

no roots,
no bole nor branch,

no memory
of shade,
of leaf,

no pollen.

NANAO SAKAKI

Memorandum

1970: Carlsbad Caverns, then I moved to
White Sands National Monument.
Dr. Albert Einstein,
government officials and the Pentagon
all watched
the mushroom-shaped cloud
right here in the Chihuahua desert
25 years ago.

1973: Jemez Springs, New Mexico,
I met a Christian priest.
At Tinian Air Base in Micronesia
he held a service for "B-29" pilots
who headed for Hiroshima,
August 6, 1945.

1945: Izumi Air Base in Yaponesia,
100 miles southeast of Nagasaki.
Three days after the Hiroshima bombing
a "B-29" due north. 30,000 feet high. 300 m.p.h.
Three minutes later
someone shouted,
"Look, Mt. Unzen's erupting!"
In the direction of Nagasaki
I saw the mushroom-shaped cloud
with my own eyes.

1946: Hiroshima. There,
one year after the bombing
I searched for

one of my missing friends.
As a substitute for him
I found a shadow man.
The atomic ray instantly
disintegrated his whole body.
all—but shadow alive
on concrete steps.

1969: Bandelier National Monument.
       Beautiful ruin
       of ancient people, the Anasazi.
       Dead of night, the earth
       quakes three times.
       Not by Jemez volcano
       but by underground nuclear explosion
       in Los Alamos.
       More ruins, more churches!

1975: The Air Base ruin in Yaponesia,
       south of Nagasaki.
       No more "Kamikaze pilots,"
       now 3,000 cranes soaring high
       in the setting sun.

1979: Northern edge of Chihuahua desert,
       Bosque del Apache National Wildlife Refuge.
       Sandhill crane, "Grus canadensis": 1,700.
       Whooping crane, "Grus americana": none.
       As a substitute
       for the extincting species
       Mr. Kerr-McGee wants to dump
       Ever-existing nuclear waste
       into "The Land of Enchantment."

JAY GRISWOLD

Origami

Spirits on the balcony at one A.M.
Two eyes are lit in the alley below
and a hiss escapes the raccoon
who has found something worth salvaging
in the garbage. He will carry it
to the nearby stream
that only flows three months a year
in a dry season.

It's a small balcony with a view
of cottonwoods the stars shine through
and a dumpster. A few leaves
have already turned the lustrous
colors of an early fall
and dangle precariously
like any word one can't find
in a cheap dictionary.

How many people does it take
to surround Rocky Flats
on a Sunday afternoon?
The day they bombed Nagasaki
was clear, blue, and the flight crew
could almost swear they heard children
singing an off-key chant to some
unknowable deity.

I think if I extend my arms
they'll rush towards me
with their strange, mutilated faces

that glow in the dark,
they'll pass into me
and go on up the lighted
pathways to the stars
like frail, paper birds

Set adrift from the windows of a hospital.
It begins to rain, a small, cold drizzle,
and a cat bristles bitterly
as the raccoon stalks by, intent
on reaching the creek before it runs out of water.
Plastic bags that were used
to cover the feet of the demonstrators
blow by in the wind.

The town sleeps peacefully.
The earth shines darkly from within.

Note: Rocky Flats, located just 16 miles from Denver, was for many years the producer of plutonium triggers used in nuclear warheads.

NANCY EIMERS

Another Kimono

So many poems with kimonos
opening darkly. Drifting over us
from the blackest corners
of touch and kiss. Kimonos
our bodies aren't worthy of
until bodies are shed
like a mottled skin that hurts
when we peel it off.
Whichever broken birdcage
my father saw clean through,
Hiroshima or Nagasaki, he
isn't too sure anymore, and you
can't hear even one wave
lap into his voice that sailed
too quietly over the ocean
and home again. You can't hear
what went into the looking
more and more finely
that rubble seldom teaches us
how to stop. How to use
each glint without wondering
what larger brightness it must have
belonged to. Each flame
on the back of the dragon
was larger and sillier
than its red tiny marvelous
angry stitches. So he bought
a black silk robe instead
and brought it home to my mother
along with his sailor hat

and a green mottled box
with a white silk lining
and rows of Japanese characters
like dancers with too many broken
arms and legs. Inside
its foreignness there was
nothing. Did she put the robe
on when they touched,
small flames burning everywhere
to forget the bitter cold
sunny afternoons, did they lie
down together and take off
everything but the bare trees
with bark dull and black
like a shining
turned in on itself?

Mervyn Clyde Witherup

b. July 14, 1910—d. May 12, 1988

Nearing the end
Father was all bones and pain.
The tumor had eaten him
Down to the rind.

Yet little he complained
Or whined. Sulphate of morphine
Eased him somewhat and he kept
His mind and wit—

Though talking was difficult.
A dry wind off the volcanic desert
Went through each of his rooms
Snuffing out cells;

Left an alkaloid crust
On his tongue. We stood by
With Sponge-On-A-Stick
When he was assaulted by thirst

And images. "Give me your hand,"
He said. "And lead me to
The water cooler. I've been
Up in the sky—I'm very tired."

Then, irritated with us,
He would ask to be left alone.
He'd suck a sponge and grab
The lifting bar; be off again

Brachiating from cloud to cloud.
"Is there a station nearby?
How do we get out of here?
You'll have to help me, son."

He died on graveyard shift.
The train came for him at 3 A.M.,
And when he ran to catch it,
He was out of breath.

Note: William Witherup's father worked for over thirty years at the Hanford Atomic Engineering Works. What began as prostate cancer in 1984 metastisized into bone marrow cancer. William Witherup has no doubt his father's cancer was Hanford related.

ROGER GREENWALD

The Half-Life of Sorrow

is about five years.
The decaying, scintillating dust
sits in the small cells of the lung
and colors your breath,
sits in the marrow and colors your blood,
sits in the bile duct.
The half-life isn't hard
to understand.
It means the sorrow
will be half gone in five years,
what's left will then take five again
to diminish by half.
So it will never stop flashing
in your life, though your life
will stop it eventually.

PREPARING THE NETS

11. Photograph used with permission from Las Vegas News Bureau.

THOMAS MCGRATH

War Resisters' Song

Come live with me and be my love
And we will all the pleasures prove—
Or such as presidents may spare
Within the decorum of Total War.

By bosky glades, by babbling streams
(Babbling of Fission, His remains)
We discover happiness' isotope
And live the half-life of our hope.

While Geiger counters sweetly click
In concentration camps we'll fuck.
Called traitors? That's but sticks and stones
We've strontium 90 in our bones!

And thus, adjusted to our lot,
Our kisses will be doubly hot—
Fornicating (like good machines)
We'll try the chances of our genes.

So (if Insufficient Grace
Hath not fouled thy secret place
Nor fall-out burnt my balls away)
Who knows? but we may get a boy—

Some paragon with but one head
And no more brains than is allowed;
And between his legs, where once was love,
Monsters to pack the future with.

SHARON DOUBIAGO

Ground Zero

for Michael Daley

I.

We met on an evening in July
in one of the old taverns of this town,
two poets, unable to write, newly arrived,
hunted and haunted. For me,
the escape. For you,
the return.

You said you would show me
the Olympic Peninsula.

The road was overgrown.
In the headlights of your car I cleared the trees.
The cabin was vandalized, gutted,
the twenty-six oddshaped windows
opening onto the Straits, Canada and all the northern sky
shot out. The sink, the pump, the stoves,
even the doors, stolen.
You wandered around, then out to the deck,
seeming to forget me in the debris.

Victoria, the only human light,
shimmered on the foreign shore.
I heard the groan of a fishing boat below the bluff,
a strange cry from the woods, like a woman,
your ex-wife, the children.

We lay on a narrow mattress in the loft,
amidst bullet shells, beer cans, mold and glass,
the cold, hard bed of delinquent teenagers.

The moon was a broken boat through the bullet shattered
    skylight.
We told each other.
First words. I said
one night stand. You said ground zero.
I said I lost my children, my lover.

You said submarine, fucking vandals.
I said kids with no place to go, kids forbidden
to love. You said holocaust. Apocalypse.
I pulled you over on me. The volcano erupted.
The world turned to ash. I screamed
love cannot be gutted.
The moon, the stars, the giant trees watched
through a bullet hole.

II.

You moved in, installed sink, stoves, water pump.
Sixty oddshaped windows. You sat here
pissed as the eagle that stared from the bluff,
the greasepen numbers on the glass around your brooding head
like cabala, some secret military code.
When I visited, I felt a vandal.
When I left you cried deserted.
Betrayed.

In November I moved in.
Sheetrock. Yellow paint named Sunlight.
My white dog, Moonlight.
I said I'd stay until the place
became a landscape in my dreams.

By moon's light through the bullet hole
I began to write.
Your words: The Duckabush, The Dosiewallips, The Hamma
    Hamma.

It snowed in December.
You followed Coyote's tracks to the log where he slept.
A trapper came on the deep path.
He had Coyote. He gave you his card.
He boasted he'd get the rest.
He hinted that for money he could get them for you.

You were not easy to love.
You couldn't speak. Your tongue was cut out.
I left, screaming down the interstate,
avoiding the road over the mountains
to my old, equally beautiful, home.
You wrote me. One Trident submarine equals
two thousand and forty Hiroshimas.

In the cities I was weighted with cedar, an inland sea,
like provisions carried on my back.
Friends I'd always respected said
they couldn't live without culture.
I was weighted with the culture of eagle, coyote, people
like weather, like stars, functions of nature, not
human will, money, concrete.

III.

I came back to study the language of gulls,
the stories they scream to each other
as they fly off their sanctuary,
Protection Island.

You pulled me up the stairs.
Beyond your head I watched the moon through the bullet hole.
You said six layers of mountains
from the road, you said rivers
without end. You quoted Rilke's
Neptune of the blood and his terrible trident.
You said Trident
submarine. You said
zero.

I came back to stare back at Eagle,
to cut, carry, and chop our firewood,
to piss in the tall fern, to shit
in *the first little house you ever built.*
I came back and broke my habit at last
of the electric typewriter.
I came back to our cruel and grinding poverty,
never enough kerosene, gasoline, postage, paper or pens.
We quit filling the propane. It is so cold in our house
the little food on our shelves is naturally iced.

I came back to listen to the woods,
gull squawk and moandance of cedar, fir and alder,
the high scream of wind through the mouth of Haro,
Rosario, Deception Pass
where the ships disappear on the inward passage.
I came back to listen to your breath
as you sleep beside me. Poet. Your words.
Puma. Ish. Milosz. The children
who once lived here.

IV.

You weighted me with your poems,
like provisions. I left, drove home.

My children were grown, gone.
Your words pulled me back.

We climb the stairs together.
The roof leaks, the cabin is for sale.
I say it is ours for now. Our one night stand,
our two hundred nights.

You tell me of this thing that is coming,
the deadliest weapon ever made.
Two football fields, four stories high.
Two thousand and forty Hiroshimas.

It can be anywhere in the world, undetected,
and hit its target within half a foot.
It can be anywhere in the world and no one,
not the President, not the Computer
will be able to find it.

One day soon it will enter the Strait of Juan de Fuca.
The most evil thing ever created
will float beneath our cabin, then down
the Hood Canal.

You say four hundred and eight cities
from a single submarine. You say
First Strike Weapon. You say
shoot out their silos. You say
USS *Ohio*.

v.

I came upon an old man
teaching his granddaughter and grandson
how to shoot.

I sat here alone.
The door banged open and four kids
burst in. Perfume, six packs, party clothes.
I think I frightened them
as much as they frightened me.

On clear days the islands rise up.
San Juan. Lopez. Orcas, white skyscrapers
on Vancouver. How many ships, my love,
have come and gone since we came? How many whales,
eagles, coyotes and gulls?
I finished my epic poem here.
You finished *The Straits*.

Every night the human city
shimmers and beckons on the Canadian shore.
Every night of one whole week
the sky wove and unwove
the rainbow flags of all the north
delicately over us. The aurora
borealis.

Two seasons of snow, now the season of light again.
My one night stand, our four hundred
nights.

I saw car lights descend Protection Island
to the water.
The leaks in the roof washed away
my nightwritten words.
We saw six killer whales
rise and fall through the water.
You said my rejected poems. I said
your smallminded editors. I said
I can almost understand now
what the gulls are saying.

VI.

My dreams take place on an inland sea,
a land soaked in silver shadow and blue.
We are traveling to the heart of the continent.
We are looking for a room to rent. We are having a baby.
We are building a house.
You say unrecognized. Unpublished. I say just
wait. You say holocaust. You say apocalypse. I say
love.

Once you went with me.
Once you came for me.

We climb the loft together. This, you say
is your home now. This northwest corner. This last place
we can run

this bed of outlaws, circle of mountains, finger
of glacier water, dark sun of winter behind
Mt. Olympus.

VII.

Light shoots through the skylights.
Twenty full moons awake us.
Moonlight sleeps below by the fire, cries from nightmare.
The Manx, the Siamese watch us through the bullet hole.
We lie in terror,
watch the giant trees arch and blow over us,
rain and wind so fierce
we wait without words to be crushed.
Finally I say maybe we should leave. You say
where would we go?
You say death like a storm that might/might not

blow over. You say Puma.
I say Tatoosh means Thunderbird.
Like Phoenix, like rebirth.
You say the last crisis is not death,
but how to be beautiful.
How to die
beautifully.

VIII.

Say the word Hiroshima.
Reflect on its meaning for one second.
Say and understand Hiroshima again.
Say and understand Hiroshima two thousand and forty times.

Assuming you are able to undersand Hiroshima
in one second, you will be able to understand Trident
in thirty four minutes. That's one Trident submarine.
To understand the destructive power of the whole
Trident fleet, it will take you seventeen hours
devoting one second to each Hiroshima. *

IX.

The real estate agents are lost on Old Dump Road.
Coyote yelps. The last hunter shoots.

The kids break through the woods
still looking for the party.
I throw open the window. "Here's your bed!
Come join us! We've kept it warm for you!"
You always pull me back to weep in your arms, where

are my teenagers?

*From Jim Douglass' Lightning East and West.

X.

The volcano erupted. The wind turned to ash.
Now the planets line up: *six hundred days and nights.*
The sun comes north
falls into the mouth of the Straits.
Rhododendron. Honeysuckle. Calypso. Trillium.
The stunted shrub blazes up
like a flaming heart.

And snow circle of mountains! Ring of fire!
Ranier, Mt. Baker, Glacier Peak, St. Helens !
Olympic Home of the Gods: *Sappho, Makah, Joyce, Quinault.*
Shi Shi, La Push, Ozette, Kalaloch.
How many nights, my love, how many poems, my great poet
we have awakened
to the low moan of a fishing boat,
someone's voice, almost,
heard in the trees

It has already left. It is on its way.
It is coming around from the other side of the continent.
The date is a secret.

It will enter the mouth of the Straits,
then slip down the Hood Canal.
It will move beneath your cabin.
It will come through your windows.

You will be anywhere in the world
and it will find you.

March 25, 1982

DAVID ROMTVEDT

Black Beauty, A Praise

On August 12, 1982, the first Trident-class submarine, the USS
Ohio, passed through the Straits of Juan de Fuca and into
Admiralty Inlet on its way to its Hood Canal home port at
Bangor, Washington. A nonviolent Peace Blockade of about fifty
people in small rowboats attempted to meet, greet, and stop the
Ohio. The Peace Blockade was turned back by ninety-eight Coast
Guard vessels sent to protect the submarine.

⇒⇐

In sub-Saharan Africa, praise poems are composed to honor a
generous superior, the attributes of an admired animal, a natural
event, a technological innovation like the bicycle or the
railroad train, or the author's valor. Clever cow thieves
sometimes compose praises to themselves. Since the penalty for
cattle thievery is immediate death, anyone who gets away with it
is generally allowed a little self-praise. Words of praise are
like water, like rain on manioc. They call for celebrating.
Usually there is dancing to accompany praising—high stepping
followed by sudden crouching, pirouetting to take aim at some
distant phantasmal creature. Sometimes praising is done in a
closed hut and the singer's friends will fire off rifles loaded
with blanks. The shots resound off the tin roof. The room
fills with smoke. Most listeners flee to the porch, choking.
But the singer keeps on singing, staring intently through the
smoke, singing praises. One who is really good can keep it up
for hours.

⇒⇐

Oh, dark Trident of the Electric Boat Yard, risen from your
    technological womb in Groton, Connecticut and dressed in
    steel, there you are, Black Beauty disguised as an Outlaw
    God or sinking angel, greetings, and

Praise as you enter the Inland Waters, the realm of the 10,000
    clouds, the home of the tongues of Ish, the protector of
    various birds. Now you come, pushing foam before your
    prow. Our farmers lie down in their fields, our fishermen
    spill their nets back into the sea, the glittering gills of the
    fish reflect light onto your dark surface,

Praise to you, and

Praise to him who takes you below for you do not sink alone, God
    though you are, you are taken below by men who, even out of
    sight, remain fully clothed.

Praise to the golden embroidery on their hats and sleeves, the
    rainbow bars on their shirt fronts, the rich woolen pants
    that warm their legs in the perpetual cool night on board,

Praise to electric lights,

Praise to the light switches,

Praise to the bulbs' brilliant glow,

Praise to everything on board and greetings Navyman, you drive
    all over the world, into the sea's deepest caverns where
    even the moon's coldest light cannot reach, from
    Vladivostok to San Diego you go,

Praise to your very quiet motors which your enemies cannot hear,
    for your way is silent, to greet all peoples equally and
    surprise them. When you shift gears and the delicate clunk
    rises to the surface, you beg pardon of the insects and
    birds and in so doing,

Praise them, the fish, the orca in their pods, the honeybees in
    late fall stumbling from monkshood to nasturtium, the crane
    flies clattering through the air in what to a human eye
    seems drunken delight, the black cormorants resting on your
    tower, invisible,

Praise, Trident-class submarine *Ohio*, elder brother to *Michigan*
    and *Florida*, those watery states,

Praise to all holders of rapid deployment death,

Praise to the stalking of death. Like the hunter who hunts not
    for the meat but for the sport, so you patrol the infinite
    drops of water, aware that both meat and death are at home,
    or at the butcher's.

Praise to your chore which is to have no chore. Only you, most
    powerful thing men have made, can wait this way with
    nothing to do, resisting boredom and error, only you, in the
    darkest green of the deepest hidden pool, at rest, testing
    your hatches and springs, assured no rivet will pop, taking
    your ease,

Praise. Far above you on the surface of the water is a tiny
    orange boat—exterior shop-grade plywood—also waiting. A
    man and woman sit in it,

Praise to these people of the eternally damp hair, hands
    wrinkled, skin soft and pale, small

Praise to them and to their small boat. And greetings too, for
    they have come to meet you, to wave their hands and offer
    loaves of bread wrapped in plastic, and stop and keep you.

Praise to bread kept safe from the sea, seaweed all around and
    edible fish, gulls, mountains that come down to the sea,
    mountains becoming the sea.

Praise to the ninety-eight boats of the Coast Guard come to clear
    your way, like a farmer who hacks down brambles with a
    machete to clear the way to an abandoned outhouse.

Praise to the red stripes on the Coast Guard boats,

Praise to the diesel smoke and fumes, helicopters in the sky,
    water cannons, fifty-caliber machine guns, M-16s and 45's
    and confusion, TV newspeople, Australians, Canadians,
    Americans, Pacific Islanders with no country but home and
    almost no home left to go to,

Praise.

Praise to community, as together we carry out this non-task, this
    withholding of power. For if you fire, and the world we
    praise explodes, and the trees shudder and fall under a hot
    sun and even the local wood rats are irradiated, then you fail,

Praise. But if somehow under some other human sun the world
    burns and you open your doors in anger, greetings, and your
    MIRVed missiles are given the gift of flight, then again,

Praise, you fail, and we do, too. So greetings to us all and

Praise, we're damp, ten thousand clouds in the sky, the tongues
    of the people cut out, hungry gull crying in the wake,

Praise, and Navyman, take her down,
                take her deep,
                take her away.

A Vigil at a Missile Silo

Because I did not marry a bomb,
nor impregnate a bomb,
nor watch a bomb swell in the belly
of a bomb,
because I did not study the bomb
in Lamaze classes,
nor watch a bomb crown and deliver and cry,
nor hold the bomb purple and cold and scared
in the bomb's white light,
nor walk the floor late at night
with the bomb sucking its bottle.

Because I do not have bombs for friends,
nor relatives, nor pets,
nor students, nor habits,
because I do not smoke the bomb
or eat it or drink it,
because I do not want to sleep with a bomb
or hear a bomb snore,
because I do not want to dream bombs
and wake sitting up, my heart a bomb.

Because I do not want bombs for neighbors,
nor have them park their bombs
in my driveway,
nor have them leave their bombs unmowed,
nor allow their bombs to bark all night.
Because I do not want to pick up
their filth,
nor bathe with the bomb

looking in the window,
or calling me on the phone,
or reading the newspaper over my shoulder,
or selling me chances in a raffle.

Because
the world should not be a bomb,
a nation should not be a bomb,
a man should not be a bomb
or have ideas that are bombs.

A bomb should not be a bomb.

ALLEN GINSBERG

Plutonian Ode

I.

What new element before us unborn in nature? Is there a new
    thing under the Sun?
At last inquisitive Whitman a modern epic, detonative, Scientific
    theme
First penned unmindful by Doctor Seaborg with poisonous hand,
    named for Death's planet through the sea beyond Uranus
whose chthonic ore fathers this magma-teared Lord of Hades, Sire
    of avenging Furies, billionaire Hell-King worshipped once
with black sheep throats cut, priest's face averted from under-
    ground mysteries in a single temple at Eleusis,
Spring-green Persephone nuptialed to his inevitable Shade, De-
    meter mother of asphodel weeping dew,
her daughter stored in salty caverns under white snow, black hail,
    gray winter rain or Polar ice, immemorable seasons before
Fish flew in Heaven, before a Ram died by the starry bush, before
    the Bull stamped sky and earth
or Twins inscribed their memories in cuneiform clay or Crab'd
    flood
washed memory from the skull, or Lion sniffed the lilac breeze in
    Eden—
Before the Great Year began turning its twelve signs, ere con-
    stellations wheeled for twenty-four thousand sunny years
slowly round their axis in Sagittarius, one hundred sixty-seven
    thousand times returning to this night

Radioactive Nemesis were you there at the beginning black Dumb
    tongueless unsmelling blast of Disillusion?

I manifest your Baptismal Word after four billion years

I guess your birthday in Earthling Night, I salute your dreadful
presence lasting majestic as the Gods,

Sabaot, Jehova, Astapheus, Adonaeus, Elohim, Iao, Ialdabaoth,
Aeon from Aeon born ignorant in an Abyss of Light,

Sophia's reflections glittering thoughtful galaxies, whirlpools of
star-spume silver-thin as hairs of Einstein!

Father Whitman I celebrate a matter that renders Self oblivion!

Grand Subject that annihilates inky hands & pages' prayers, old
orators' inspired Immortalities,

I begin your chant, openmouthed exhaling into spacious sky over
silent mills at Hanford, Savannah River, Rocky Flats, Pantex,
Burlington, Albuquerque

I yell thru Washington, South Carolina, Colorado, Texas, Iowa,
New Mexico,

where nuclear reactors create a new Thing under the Sun, where
Rockwell war-plants fabricate this death stuff trigger in ni-
trogen baths,

Hanger-Silas Mason assembles the terrified weapon secret by ten
thousands, & where Manzano Mountain boasts to store

its dreadful decay through two hundred forty millennia while our
Galaxy spirals around its nebulous core.

I enter your secret places with my mind, I speak with your pres-
ence, I roar your Lion Roar with mortal mouth.

One microgram inspired to one lung, ten pounds of heavy metal
dust adrift slow motion over gray Alps

the breadth of the planet, how long before your radiance speeds
blight and death to sentient beings?

Enter my body or not I carol my spirit inside you, Unapproachable
Weight,

O heavy heavy Element awakened I vocalize your consciousness to
six worlds

I chant your absolute Vanity. Yeah monster of Anger birthed in fear
O most

Ignorant matter ever created unnatural to Earth! Delusion of
metal empires!

Destroyer of lying Scientists! Devourer of covetous Generals, In-
cinerator of Armies & Melter of Wars!

Judgment of judgments, Divine Wind over vengeful nations, Mo-
lester of Presidents, Death-Scandal of Capital politics! Ah civ-
ilizations stupidly industrious!

Canker-Hex on multitudes learned or illiterate! Manufactured
Spectre of human reason! O solidified imago of practitioners
in Black Arts

I dare your Reality, I challenge your very being! I publish your
cause and effect!

I turn the Wheel of Mind on your three hundred tons! Your name
enters mankind's ear! I embody your ultimate powers!

My oratory advances on your vaunted Mystery! This breath dispels
your braggart fears! I sing your form at last

behind your concrete & iron walls inside your fortress of rubber &
translucent silicon shields in filtered cabinets and baths of
lathe oil,

My voice resounds through robot glove boxes & ingot cans and
echoes in electric vaults inert of atmosphere,

I enter with spirit out loud into your fuel rod drums underground
on soundless thrones and beds of lead

O density! This weightless anthem trumpets transcendent
through hidden chambers and breaks through iron doors
into the Infernal Room!

Over your dreadful vibration this measured harmony floats audi-
ble, these jubilant tones are honey and milk and wine-sweet
water

Poured on the stone block floor, these syllables are barley groats I
scatter on the Reactor's core,

I call your name with hollow vowels, I psalm your Fate close by, my
breath near deathless ever at your side

to Spell your destiny, I set this verse prophetic on your mausoleum
walls to seal you up Eternally with Diamond Truth! O
doomed Plutonium.

II.

The Bard surveys Plutonian history from midnight lit with Mer-
    cury Vapor streetlamps till in dawn's early light
he contemplates a tranquil politic spaced out between Nations'
    thought-forms proliferating bureaucratic
& horrific arm'd, Satanic industries projected sudden with Five
    Hundred Billion Dollar Strength
around the world same time this text is set in Boulder, Colorado
    before front range of Rocky Mountains
twelve miles north of Rocky Flats Nuclear Facility in United States
    on North America, Western Hemisphere
of planet Earth six months and fourteen days around our Solar Sys-
    tem in a Spiral Galaxy
the local year after Dominion of the last God nineteen hundred
    seventy eight
Completed as yellow hazed dawn clouds brighten East, Denver
    city white below
Blue sky transparent rising empty deep & spacious to a morning
    star high over the balcony
above some autos sat with wheels to curb downhill from Flatiron's
    jagged pine ridge,
sunlit mountain meadows sloped to rust-red sandstone cliffs above
    brick townhouse roofs
as sparrows waked whistling through Marine Street's summer
    green leafed trees.

III.

This ode to you O Poets and Orators to come, you father Whitman
    as I join your side, you Congress and American people,
you present meditators, spiritual friends & teachers, you O Master
    of the Diamond Arts,
Take this wheel of syllables in hand, these vowels and consonants
    to breath's end

take this inhalation of black poison to your heart, breathe out this
    blessing from your breast on our creation
forests cities oceans deserts rocky flats and mountains in the Ten
    Directions pacify with this exhalation,
enrich this Plutonian Ode to explode its empty thunder through
    earthen thought-worlds
Magnetize this howl with heartless compassion, destroy this
    mountain of Plutonium with ordinary mind and body
    speech,
thus empower this Mind-guard spirit gone out, gone out, gone be-
    yond, gone beyond me, Wake space, so Ah!

JOHN BRANDI

Preparing the Nets at New Stuyahok

Break the law!
Climb the windy forefront and
burn in the snow.

Chant the oldtime song
and melt like ice
off Nunivak.

Mend and lower the nets
of revolution.

Let the men who say
bombing makes sense be served
infinity's harsh illusion.

Let them die
in the distance between the countries
they have eyes on.

DAVID MCKAIN

Opening Day

Gusts of wind cruise like fish
through bare branches of oak and dogwood
by the river. I've come here to read
a letter from a friend locked up in prison,
trying to understand how he has found the heart
to write about cowbirds singing at his shoulder,
about seagulls flying upriver.

The damp air smells like a bucket
half-buried in leafmold—rusted out,
filled with bullet holes and earthworms.
He writes they have a garden where
they grow their own corn and tomatoes,
leaving plenty for the deer and woodchuck.

One Sunday morning he skipped Mass
to dig worms and cut a fishing pole
while the cook smuggled in a jug of wine—
the guard, a few sticks of dry kindling.
Then the three of them squatted in a circle
behind the tool shed, coaxing a spark
from the wet leaves, feasting in the drizzle.

Months earlier, in court, a reporter asked
why he had sprayed "Auschwitz" on a u.s. Trident,
hammering its nose cone. At first he shrugged,
as though everyone knew the answer, but then,
in the same quiet voice of the letter, bemused,
he smiled and said, To make a dent in history.

I carry the crumpled letter in my wallet
to remember what it's like to be angry—
angry enough to smuggle paint and a hammer
into an airshow; plant corn and tomatoes;
drink wine; walk in the mist before anyone
else gets up, the seagulls yammering upriver.

JOSEPH BRUCHAC

Wahsah Zeh (War Dance)
—As Long as the Grass

Then Old Man spoke to the people.
"Go and hide in our Mother," he said.
"The wind which comes will blow away your breath.
The rain which comes will burn your flesh.
Go and hide in our Mother," he said.

A cool morning in April.
I drive to work thinking.
The tiny fists of buds begin
to swell on trees beside the road.
The sap in the maple buckets turns yellow.
The grass edges its way to green.
These are things which can be seen,
but other forces touch my life,
more invisible than air itself
or greed which masters human hearts.

Woman who fell from the sky
    Grandmother
Woman who fell from the sky
    Grandmother

Who held the seeds of plants in her hand
Who fell to new earth on Turtle's back
Who held the good seeds of plants in her hand
Who fell to the Earth on Turtle's back

You, who gave birth, your children need you
You, who gave life, your grandchildren need you

You, who brought birth, your grandchildren need you
You, who brought life, your children need you

Less than 500 miles from here,
men and women work calmly near the Nuclear Plant.
They tell themselves, as they tell reporters,
that nothing is wrong, that American know-how
which sends rockets streaking, scrawls of chalk
across black space to distant planets,
can always control the monsters it creates.

They do not know the stories
of the Earth they live on,
have never heard of the Evil Mind
Longhouse People tell of in winterlodge tales.

They have never seen the Kinzua Dam
cover good corn land of the Seneca Nation,
graves of leaders, George Washington's word.

They have never seen Smallpox
smile from gift blankets,
seen beaches of Maui, Kaui and Hawaii
covered with 400,000 bodies,
limbs burned by the fire of western disease . . .
as the Mandan, Arikara enter the Sweat Lodge
and the pustules swell, swell up like a bubble
of radioactive hydrogen trapped
within the dome of a safe reactor.

And perhaps this nation knows no myths
and even the story of Mary Shelley's haunted flesh
means nothing more than a way to hold children
for an hour before the pale eye of commerce
whose rainbow dreams hypnotize away
all humanity which does not exist for profit.

And somehow
no one knows how
Karen Silkwood's car
goes off the road.
A thousand papers flutter about her,
they are the white swans who flew up from the water
to catch the woman who fell from the sky.
They are too late.

And somehow
no one knows how
when police arrive
the papers are gone
and the men of Kerr-McGee sleep soundly
and the red earth of Oklahoma
is Karen Silkwood's burying ground.

And somehow
no one knows how
there was plutonium contamination
in her bathroom
plutonium contamination
in her bedroom
plutonium contamination
in her food and perhaps
say the men at the Nuclear Plant
whose safety practices she had condemned
she intended to contaminate herself
to gain publicity
this is what they say
the men at Kerr-McGee
and do they sleep soundly?

This is a song of quiet anger,
of anger which will be quiet no longer.

If only, perhaps, they could watch just one finger
of their left hand begin to decay half an inch,
a tenth of an inch each time they absorbed
enough to shorten a life,
start the crazy quilt proliferation of leucocytes.
If only *that*, instead of numbers,
of dosimeter readings which measure a "4"
which they say is only as much radiation
as one would get from 200 chest x-rays.
Then they set "5" as the number safe
to absorb in one month.

Madame Curie,
patron saint
of luminous watches,
we honor you.

Madame Curie,
held up to me,
heroine of my childhood,
we honor you.

Madame Curie,
limbs thin as sticks,
hair falling out,
we honor you.

Because the spirit cannot be seen,
is it not there?
Tell me it is not there
when you see the body
of a human
which no longer holds it.
Tell me that breath is less important
than the color of skin, the clothing you wear,
the whiteness of teeth in a "sex-appeal" smile.

Woman who comes walking
  Grandmother
Woman who comes walking
  Grandmother

You wear a dress of white Buffalo Skin
You walk to us with visible breath
You wear the dress of white Buffalo Skin
You walk to us from four directions

White Buffalo Woman
White Buffalo Woman
White Buffalo Woman
White Buffalo Woman

You bring the Pipe,
the heart of the people
You bring the stone
the blood of the people
You bring the stem
the plants of the earth
You bring the tobacco
breath of the Creator

And of those who saw you coming
one whose heart was good
brought back life to the people,
one whose heart was bad,
who saw your body and not the beauty
of the gift you carried
who looked at you as corporations
look at the Earth, at the coal of Black Mesa,
at the oil shale of the Crow Reservation
at the North Slope of Alaska,
that one, that other one

fell to the Earth
fell to the Earth
to the Earth as bones
and worms crawled among his bones.

This is a song of anger
for the dream they are killing
is not just my own.
They eat the earth from beneath the feet
of our grandchildren's grandchildren.

Satanta, the great Kiowa chief,
said it more than a hundred years ago.
"You cut down the trees, kill the Buffalo,
you make the streams filthy
so that even you have no water to drink.
Are you people crazy?"
And in answer the army officers spat at his feet.

Let them kill themselves?
Is that what you say?
But the grave they dig is American,
a giant economy size, a family model,
the only product manufactured for profit
which does not have built-in obsolescence.

The half-life of radioactive wastes
manufactured by our nuclear plants
can be measured in tens of thousands of years.
The glaciers returned to the poles
but those will remain, faithful through the ages.

It is as if the poison which killed a Roman emperor
stayed in the air until today, killing every person
who breathed it.

It is as if the spear which wounded the side
of Christ still hung, invisible, on the hill
of Golgotha, goring every living creature
which came close to that place.

It is as if the stone Cain hurled
against his brother were orbiting, a tiny evil moon,
striking down guilty and innocent from that time on.

And the Sun
watches

We do not see him.
We do not accept the gift offered freely.
There is no profit in solar power.
There is power in the reactor's poison.
There is profit in oil, in coal, in the rape
of our Mother to bring forth her black blood
and bones burning in factories, smoke choking sky
acid rain weeping into mountain lakes,
trout dying, trees dying, the water bitter.

And Grandmother Moon
fills up the night,
Grandmother Moon fills even our dreams
with the light of Sun
the light they have not seen

A man is about to leap from a ledge.
He is not trying to kill himself.
He swears he will be able to fly.
Some believe him, some know
he is a fool, but no one stops him.
They all stand by
as he leaps to the crowded street below,

even though, strapped to his back
as if it could lift him into flight,
is a case of dynamite.

This poem is a poem of anger.
This poem calls back those of the past.
It calls back Powhatan
it calls back Madakwando
it calls back Pontiac
it calls back Tecumseh
it calls back Dragging Canoe
it calls back Osceola
it calls back Captain Jack
it calls back Chief Joseph
it calls back Cochise
it calls back Dull Knife
it calls back Satank
it calls back Looking Glass
it calls back Crazy Horse
it calls back Sitting Bull

Tatanka Iyotake
Tatanka Iyotake
Tatanka Iyotake
Tatanka Iyotake

It calls all those whose spirits never left us
It calls all those whose spirits never left us
It calls all those whose spirits never left us
It calls all those whose spirits never left us

GER O NI MO
GER O NI MO
GER O NI MO
GER O NI MO

There are no mountains in which to hide
from the rain which will fall.
No one can dodge the bullets of this gun
which kills even the hand which fires it.

This poem calls back Ayontwantha.
This poem calls back the Peacemaker.
This poem will say the sacred names.
It calls all those who love the Earth,
calls both living and dead on Turtle's back.

It calls the Bear Mothers
It calls Gluskabe
It calls Grandmother Spider
It calls Manabozho
It calls Coyote
It calls Moon, our Grandmother
It calls the Manitous
It calls the Thunderbird
It calls the Kachinas
It calls the Thunderers

HE NO
HE NO
HE NO
HE NO

Grandfathers
wash the Earth
Grandmothers
wash the minds
of those who do not believe in circles

Grandfathers, take them,
make their minds straight

Grandmothers, take them,
make their hearts good.

Listen, all of us who love our children
Listen, all of us who love our land
Listen, all of us who love our parents
Listen, all of us who love our friends

All of us are "Indian" now
The treaty not made is the only one
which might never be broken.
It promises waste, it promises death
for as long as the rivers run
for as long as the grass shall grow

We must answer: No.
We must answer: No.
We must answer: No.
WE MUST ANSWER: NO!!!!

PATRICIA GOEDICKE

Shadow

I say to You Halt
I say to You Stop It
This is not the way to go
Your body has shriveled up
That used to loom at us like thunder
Your body is nothing but an echo
That used to shine at us like a hydrofoil
Striding over the sea
I say to You nothing is safe anymore
Not even breath
I say to You we are drying up
I say to You we have raisins for souls
Even when I drop mine into water
It won't swell, I say to You *No wings, No wings*
And You made us
Not even humor seems to be able to elevate us,
What is that strange stink in the air
Is it gas? Is it radioactive? Is it safe?
No wonder people think I'm crazy
Up here on the rooftops waving my megaphone
Stop shouting, they tell me
Go back to your knitting, milk your own veins
And forget about ours, we have our own rows to ruin

But the stairs I'm standing on are folding
And theirs too,
You better listen to me, Shadow
What goes up must come down
This morning I woke up muttering
Speak to me in lilies but I'm not a lily

I'm sick, I'm a dead prune
Why did You dress us in petals
In the first place, turning on our stems
Like numb barber poles blubbering
He loves me, He loves me not
When I go under for the last time, when the air
Slides out of me like a fishing line or a trombone
That won't stop,
What have You given me to hold onto,
You said it was our fault
And it is but then You left us
Why did you close Your mouth at us
In the name of all the little dried apricots
And babies, especially the babies
When the great blast of holocaust cracks the sky
And the book of the world wide open
I say to You Halt
I say to You Stop It
This is no way to go
I'm talking to You, Shadow

PRAYER FOR CONTINUATION

12. Photograph by Arthur Sasse. Permission granted by UPI/Bettmann.

Psalm

That from the seed of men
No man,
And from the seed of the olive tree
No olive tree
Shall grow,
This must be measured
With the yardstick of death.

Those who live
Beneath the earth
In cement spheres,
Their strength is
A blade of grass
Lashed by snow.

The desert is history.
Termites write it
Into sand
With their pincers.

And no one will inquire
About a species
Eager
For self-destruction.

translated from the German
by Daniel Simko

WILLIAM WITHERUP

The Lamb of Peace, The Ram of War

Barbarians sweep down from the Carpathians,
Iron helmets casting sharp shadows.
Swordsmen disembowel the moon
And raise up Christ and Lenin
In rituals of lightning and sperm.

Blitzkrieg: warriors smear their foreheads
And lintels with vaginal blood,
Their spear tips with uranium.
They build cities of assassination
At the mouth of every river.

Liars, murderers, thugs—
They appoint Yahweh head of CIA,
Implant tracking devices into foetuses.
Rasputin drops his pants at dinner,
Says, "*This* is the Tsar of Mother Russia!"
Are you washed in the blood of the ram?

The lamb, the calf and the wolf cub
Lie down together, panting,
Waiting for the skies to heal;
Wary of the missile phalanxes
Flashing above the trampled wheat.

Within the cities of assassination
Blind children
Try crayon drawings of the moon.

BERYLE WILLIAMS

Strategies for Survival
(for the post-nuclear children)

Our fossilized bones
some day may lie
slipped scarcely beneath
the dark upper loam
of earth, "finds"
for the children
with gilt hair
and body suits of gold mail
or some fine fabric made
possible by the discovery
of that one fail-safe element.

Old body
be determined
to leave nothing but dust
for these sun-charmed children.

Bones are nothing
but messages
saying repeat me, love me
back into shape
that I was, clacking
their fleshless way
into the hearts
of children born forgetting
they have them.

Crumble, bones, scatter
gnash yourselves to nothing
like teeth of fitful sleepers

do not claim what you were
nor offer yourselves up
for inspection
rejection
collection
and especially not for
loving reconstruction.
The world has had enough
of love—it often breeds
and feeds such moral
hates.

Better, we say, to leave
these wandering children
wandering

than to trip them up
with absurd old relics of a kind
that destroyed itself
for love
of too much
or perhaps
of too little
in too great amounts but nevertheless
for love.

Better, we say (in the dark, and only
when our own children sleep)
to leave no trace
that might entice
that one slightly curious

star-eyed drifter
(too like these vulnerable ones
we've known) away from aimless
careless drifting—better,
we whisper—and dream
separately
secretly
of arrows on rocks, scripts in caves,
bulges in earth just strange enough
to tempt a digger, leave clues
all through the restless night
until children, bright-faced
and gilt-haired in sunlight
wake these late sleepers
to morning.

Prayer for Men and Children

Men sleep
with loose hands that by day are fists
holding fear.
Men sleep and women are awake
because some men are dreaming
cobalt blue, the slowest death
carried by wind
and pure rain looking innocent.
Grandmothers feel this in their bones.
Aunts weep for no good reason.
Mothers guard windows of sand-blown houses
where men and children sleep.

This is a prayer that enters a house
and touches a lantern to light.
For the sleeping men and gentle work
of women. Their hands wash dishes in pans
silent as breath.
They touch water
and dream out the window
toward lost voices of children.
At the window bottles have changed violet.
Pale linen is blowing on the lines.

This is a prayer to save the soft gray dresses
of evening, blowing suddenly off the lines
of their bodies. To save the eyes
that watched flowers on wallpaper
ignite like a thousand suns.
A fire wind. A prayer against heat

that burns dark roses from shirts into skin
because fire passes first through the dark.
Newspapers held casually
write a day's history
across the sleepless faces of women.

Burning, another world enters
through the shadows of bodies
flashed on walls,
the dark wedges between blue fingers
that were praying for sleeping men and children.

NAOMI SHIHAB NYE

Shoulders

A man crosses the street in rain,
stepping gently, looking two times north and south,
because his son is asleep on his shoulder.

No car must splash him.
No car drive too near to his shadow.

This man carries the world's most sensitive cargo
but he's not marked.
Nowhere does his jacket say FRAGILE,
HANDLE WITH CARE.

His ear fills up with breathing.
He hears the hum of a boy's dream
deep inside him.

We're not going to be able
to live in this world
if we're not willing to do what he's doing
with one another.

The road will only be wide.
The rain will never stop falling.

ALICIA OSTRIKER

An Army of Lovers

we know each other
by secret symbols,

though, remote, speechless,
we pass each other on the pavement
. . . . .
we nameless initiates,
born of one mother
—H.D., "The Walls Do Not Fall"

Half sleeping, for she has been traveling
And should sleep, she takes her pen and writes
"'An army of lovers cannot fail,' Plato,
The Symposium. No ammunition,
No purple hearts. We can salute each other
By a long gaze. None of us is alone."

She thinks, "I am writing this letter with my blood
And estrogen, true ink,"
And drops the pen. Can a dream appear so real
You think you can chew it like steak?
Hit into it like the leather punching bag
In the downtown gymnasium,
Never getting exhausted?

She brushes her teeth, puts on her nightgown,
Crawls into bed. She is remembering
The man in the three piece suit, the flight from Houston,
His saying "Nuke 'em" to her, flashing
An oilman's smile.

She watched him watch the movie *Jaws*.
She drank her gin and tonic and wondered
What it was really like, being attacked by a shark.
There is a cover of *Hustler* that has burned
A portion of her brain forever. A busty girl
Is being fed, from the waist down, into
A hamburger grinder: you are supposed to laugh.
Dear Lord, she is so tired.

She has filled her folders and cubbyholes of her desk with
    evidence
Photos of flyspecked children, miners gaunt
With emphysema, butchered girls. She thinks
She is like Abraham bargaining with God
On a bare hill outside of Sodom. A thousand
Innocent dead is too many. Five is too many. One is too many.
They shall not hurt nor destroy, a wire twangs in her mind,
Her bargaining position. She falls asleep,
The world aflame and she wants
Not a hair scorched,
She wants everyone to escape.

She falls asleep. And what does she do when the dream
Of an army of lovers becomes her own arm
Burning in every tendon to hold a torch
In the face of that Houston man, to melt it away?
Oh see, her cheeks are wet. Let her friend waken
Warm under their blankets, aware of something wrong.
Let the friend stroke her hair and shoulders, and hug her
Until they both sleep, ink on their writers' fingers.

SUSAN GRIFFIN

Prayer for Continuation

I.

There is a record
I wish to make here.
A life.
And not this life alone
but the thread
which keeps shining
like the gold floss woven into cloth
which catches your eyes
and you are won over.

Kyrie Eleison
Baruch Atah
Hosana Adonai
Omne Padme Gloria
Nam Myo-Ho
Renge Kyo
Galan
galancillo.
Do you love
this world?

Where is the point I can enter?
Where is the place I can touch?

Let me tell you
I am so serious
and taking aim
like a woman with a bow
eyes looking silently

at each space between the trees
for movement.

II.

I cannot begin now.
I do not wish to write these numbers
on this page here.
224 warheads destroy
every Soviet city with a population
over 100,000.
But once I begin writing
the figures do not stop.
A 20 megaton
bomb, a firestorm rages over
3,000 acres.
A 1,000 megaton bomb
destroys California
Nevada, Utah, Oregon,
Puget Sound.
Destroys.
California.

III.

Thirty-seven days from my
fortieth birthday. I have
gone up and down this coast
so many times I could trace
the shape of it for you
with my hands, up
into the high cold trees, down
to warm water and
the sprawling city

where I was
born, 1943.
In that year
while I slept
not entirely wanted
in a still room
behind Venetian blinds
somewhere in a foreign language
babies were set on fire.
Their cries did not wake me.
Only I breathed in the dust
of their deaths.

IV.

It is my love I hold back
hide
not wanting to be seen
scrawl of hand
writing
don't guess
don't guess at my
passion
a wholly wild and raging
love for this world.

V

(Home)

If you look in this block
in the North of California
you will find a house
perhaps a century old

with the original wood shingles
dark from years of sun
and fine old joints, the men
who made them are dead, the attic
made into a bedroom now, the
linoleum added in 1955.
Twenty years ago
I lived there, a student
studying the history of
Western Civilization, reading John Milton,
looking out the attic window
at a cement sidewalk
which was before just a
dirt path
and Spanish, and was before
perhaps, a forest or a
meadow, a field,
belonging to the Ohlone
who have all
even their children
even all traces of who they were
perished.

VI.

This is the world I was born into.
Very young I learned
my mother and my father
had a terrible sorrow.
And very young
I learned this sorrow from them.

VII.

The mind is vast

what we know small.
Do you think we are not all
sewn together?
I still argue with her
grit my teeth trying to feel
the pain that riddled her body
the day they told her
she would never walk.
I try to enter her mind
the night she took her own life.

Cells have memory!
I shout to her.
Science gave you
an unnecessary despair.

VIII.

Nor do they argue
nor do they understand
nor do they know
but still it is so.
And there are structures of
unknowing
we call disbelief.

IX.

Every American city
with a population above
25,000
targeted.
A bomb with the
explosive power

13. Photograph used with permission from Los Alamos National Laboratory.

of 20 million tons of TNT.
80 per cent of all cancers.
How is it,
this woman asks,
the brilliant efforts of
American scientists
have been put
to such destructive uses?

x.

It is not real, they tell us,
this home we long for
but a dream of a place
that never
existed.
But it is so familiar!
And the longing in us is
ourselves.

xi.

This is the world I was born into.
I saw the wave and its white curl.
I saw branches coming from trees
like streams from rivers.
And the water poisoned
and the land.
I saw the whale leap out of the water
I saw my child's eyes come out of me
                    her first cry.
And the air, the rain acid.

Kyrie Eleison
Baruch Atah

Hosana
Adonai
Do you love the world?

XII.

Suppose she lay down her bow.
And went into
that place
stepping so slowly
so surely.

XIII.

This is what I wanted to tell you.
This is what I wanted to say.
Words come late and dark
near sleep.
She said to me
my head was eating my heart.
And what is good?
What is bad?
The delicacy of transmission.
Old alliances fracture
like the cold branches of a
winter tree.
This is the closest I can get.
The world is washed in space.
It is the words she used
precisely those
and I could not remember them.
Only my conviction.
There was badness and goodness.
One was bad.
The other suffered.

And I wanted to mend her.
She told me the whole story
and I told her what was
good and what was bad,
and this was not what she needed.
You think I am trying
to throw away morality
but I am not.
I am not trying to
throw away caring.
In a dream
I see myself
a handsome man
walking without feeling
into a desert.
I am not like him
yet this dream comes to me
and I feel grief.
Out at the edge of this territory
is a missile.
I know for certain
this weapon is bad.
I do not try to mend her
and this makes me weep
for what she has suffered.

XIV.

(The Enemy)
I wanted you to be good.
I wanted your judgments.
But all your rules became ash.
Your goodness was like an island.
(Your sainthood was the sin.)
Now that you have fallen
I cross the water

wrestle with you
charge you to bless me
watch as you
appear and disappear
become me.

XV.

The mind is vast.
A whale blows.
Shall we pitch ourselves into terror?
Shall we come home?
Enter darkness, weep
know the dimension
of absence, the unreachable deep.

XVI.

How far can they go?
This is my speech
an American speech of whalers
and farmers what my
people did
plain, simple, honed
to the point
how far will they go?
Is there a stopping point?
Everyone knows there is not.

XVII.

What can we make of this?
Two children held hostage together
in a van
for ten months.

What kind of man?
A girl, born three years ago
in California,
a boy who was born in
and survived Vietnam.
How far?
The children were continually beaten
with a rubber hose
and forced into sexual acts
in exchange for being fed.
I am a woman
who reads this story
in a newspaper.

XVIII.

(Bone Cancer)

You must not let terror overtake you.
It is a bone breaking in the middle of the night.
It is a misspelled word.
It is everything you thought you knew
becoming unknown, the leaves
stripped from the tree,
all the greenness orange and dry,
it is pain past bearable, you must not.
Down the street in the darkness someone young
is dying. The soil, perhaps under your feet
is poison, the water you drink.
What is this? Be reasonable. Disaster
is always predicted and look
we exist. Humanity had a day of birth,
slow, unreasoned, surprising. Now,
is it possible, is it possible
could this be?

XIX.

Do we not want
this place
to find it
the body again
hearth, heart.
How is it I can say this
so that you will
see too what I have seen.
After the fires
(after the unspeakable)
there will be no home.
And what of us
will remain in memory?
Nothing?

XX.

At least we think of them.
The six million.
We long for them.
Want them to be like they were
before
want the music
their mothers and fathers sang
to pass from our lips.
And we ask
How is it they did not know?

XXI.

Do you think it is right
to despair?
No, no, it is not about
right and wrong.

It is the thread
shining.

XXII.

Kyrie Eleison
Baruch Atah Adonai
Omne Padme
New rules
take the place of the old.
Be Here Now
is the lesson.
But I do not want to be.
I am one hundred years away
into the future.
My heart is wondering.
Will this old tree grow even bigger?
Will its roots threaten the foundation of
                                                    this house?
Will there be a daughter of a
       daughter of a daughter
       a son? And what is the
look in their eyes? Tell me
what you see there. And
do you like to watch
them as they walk across
fields.

Fields?

ELIZABETH SPIRES

Sunday Afternoon at Fulham Palace

Putney Bridge, London

A Sunday afternoon in late September, one of the last
good weekends before the long dark, old couples
taking the air along the Thames, sunning themselves,
their arms and legs so pale, *exposed,*
eyes closed against the slanting autumn light,
while the young press forward, carry us
along in the crowd to the fair at Fulham Palace
where a few people have already spread blankets and tablecloths
for the picnics they've brought, laughing and talking
as they wait for the music to begin at three o'clock.
Inside the palace gates, a man inflates
a room-size, brightly painted rubber castle,
the children impatiently waiting for the walls and turrets to go up,
the spongy floor they like to jump on.
The palace is empty. The Bishop gone.
Now overfed goldfish swim slowly round and round
in the crumbling courtyard fountain, and farther on,
a white peacock stands still as a statue,
still as a stone, whether in pride or sorrow
at being the last of its kind here I don't know.
A low door opens into the Bishop's walled garden, but once
inside nothing miraculous or forbidden tempts us,
just a few flowers and herbs among weeds
(unlike those illuminated scenes in books of hours),
the past passing away too quickly to catch or recognize.

Out on the other side, we pick our way
among booths put up for the day,

one woman, predictably, passing out pamphlets
on nuclear winter and cruise missiles, as if she could stop it alone.
The Fulham Band takes its place on the platform,
the conductor announcing as the overture,
"Those Magnificent Men in Their Flying Machines,"
the crossed shadow of coincidence, of airplanes from Gatwick
passing over at two-minute intervals, touching us
for a moment before they fly into the day's
unplanned pattern of connections, the music
attracting more of a crowd, men, women, and children
making their entrances like extras in a movie,
in pairs, in families, no one alone that I can see
except one girl, no more than ten,
lagging behind the others, lost completely
in a vivid, invisible daydream until her mother finds her,
brings her back with a touch on the arm,
and the daughter says, unbelievably,
"I was thinking about what kind of anesthesia
they'll give me when I have my first baby."

The future expands, then contracts, like an eye's iris
    opening and closing,
walling me into a room where light and sound come and go,
first near, then far, as if I had vertigo.
It is easy, too easy, to imagine the world ending
on a day like today, the sun shining and the band playing,
the players dreamily moving now into Ellington's "Mood Indigo."
Easy to see the great gray plane hovering briefly overhead,
the gray metal belly opening and the bomb dropping,
a flash, a light "like a thousand suns,"
and then the long winter.
The white peacock. Erased. The goldfish in the fountain
swimming crazily as the water boils up around them, evaporates.
The children's castle. Gone. The children. The mothers
    and the fathers.

As if a hand had suddenly erased a huge blackboard.
Thank God you don't know what I'm thinking.
You press my hand as if to ask, "Am I here with you?
Do you want to go?" pulling me back to this moment,
to this music we are just coming to know, the crowd around us
growing denser, just wanting to live their lives,
each person a *nerve,* thinking and feeling
too much as sensation pours over them
in a ceaseless flow, the music, as we move to go,
jumping far back in time, the conductor oddly choosing
something devotional, a coronet solo
composed, and probably played here, by Purcell
      three centuries ago.
All is as it was as we make our way back along the Thames
to Putney Bridge, the old souls still sleeping unaware,
hands lightly touching, as the river bends in a gentle arc
around them. Mood indigo. The white peacock.
The walled garden and the low door.
As if, if it did happen, we could bow our heads
and ask, once more, to enter that innocent first world.

C.D. WRIGHT

On the Eve of Our Mutually Assured Destruction

We were not even moving. No one was moving.
We had the windows rolled
so we could hear. No one was hurt. They
were working on the bridge. A woman
held the sign: men working. The radio was beat.
Somebody must have ripped off the aerial
in the lot. Wednesday, March 6: wind shovelling fog.
We were talking about going to another place . . .
until the worst was over . . . where insects nest
in the ears of convolvuli, clear soups are imbibed.
We didn't have change. Not a bill.
After the bridge came the tunnel, then
the toll. We felt so lonesome we wanted to cry.
The couple ahead of us lit up.
Their baby thrashed in its carrier.
We talked about following
the migration of protected beings.
We wanted to leap or turn around. There
could be no turning around. We would get rid
of the chairs and the stoneware. Find a home
for the black mollies. We would rent
bicycles in an old town under a machicolated wall.
Clatter over cobbles in public health specs
arguing about Trotsky. Like thirties' poets.
Yes there would be the dense canopy,
the floor of mosses, liverworts and ferns.
I would open my legs like a book
letting the soft pencils of light

fall on our pages, like doors
into a hothouse, cereus blooming there.
I would open up like a wine list, a mussel, wings
to be mounted without tearing.
I would part my legs in the forest
and let the fronds impress themselves in the resin
of my limbs; smoothe your rump
like a horse's. To wit the whole world would not be lost.

Prayer for a Future Beyond
Ideology and War

When the world dissolves in its own chemicals
And the people's bodies are as ghostly as the particles
    discovered by Josephson in 1962, which pass through walls
    like light through air,
And the people's buildings are born again as blueprints, and the
    print is invisible and the blue is the blue of the innocent,
    amnesiac sea,
And the hardwood trees, falling in forests everywhere, their
    fractured branches tangled like a woman's hair after love,
    make no sound not because they are not heard but because
    there is no longer anything for them to land on and thud
    against
(The pine trees like unplayed whole notes trapped in a barbed-
    wire stave)—

And even the stones have become as insubstantial as
thought—

May there be new cities in the tolerant sky,
Held in place by their own gravity
(Or lack of it), places of peace where a man and a woman
Holding each other in the familiar bed of their long night
May see, through the window, as clear as light
The stubbornly loving shadow of a star that was once our sun.

14. Photograph used with permission from Los Alamos National Laboratory.

Destruction

The universe is forever falling apart—
No need to push the button,
It collapses at a finger's touch:
Why, it barely hangs on the tail of a sparrow's eye.

The universe is so much eye secretion,
Hordes leap from the tips
Of your nostril hairs. Lift your right hand:
It's in your palm. There's room enough
On the sparrow's eyelash for the whole.

A paltry thing, the universe:
Here is all strength, here the greatest strength.
You and the sparrow are one
And, should he wish, he can crush you.
The universe trembles before him.

> translated from the Japanese by Lucien Stryk,
> with Takashi Ikemoto

Explosion

I'm an unthinking dog,
a good-for-nothing cat,
a fog over gutter,
a blossom-swiping rain.

I close my eyes, breathe—
radioactive air! A billion years
and I'll be shrunk to half,
pollution strikes my marrow.

So what—I'll whoop at what
remains. Yet scant blood left,
reduced to emptiness by nuclear
fission, I'm running very fast.

translated from the Japanese by Lucien Stryk,
with Takashi Ikemoto

Simultaneously

Simultaneously, five thousand miles apart,
two telephone poles, shaking and roaring
and hissing gas, rose from their emplacements
straight up, leveled off and headed
for each other's land, alerted radar
and ground defense, passed each other
in midair, escorted by worried planes,
and plunged into each other's place,
steaming and silent and standing straight,
sprouting leaves.

PAMELA USCHUK

Of Simple Intent

The desert can be all things to man;
but above all is a symbol of what has
been most deeply denied in man's own
spirits . . . a bright mirror wherein they
see the arid reflection of their own
rejected and uncared-for selves.
                        —Laurens van der Post

Sunset fires the San Pedro Valley—
here, mountains are ancient and cryptic
as primordial tongues
comfortable in this thirsty world
our words are useless to describe.
What they tell us is like a stone
of simple intent in our hands.
                                    In inescapable heat
light is the mirror that charges
each pitch of land and season.
Who would call this place barren cannot know
the endurance of Live Oak,
Manzanita,
flowering Mesquite
or whole nations of wildflowers
that thrive among rocks after rain.

We are house-weary
tired of the same news—
                            mass murderers, terrorists, shifting
Middle East wars, soaring

defense budgets to create doomsday weapons
that can detonate the world from outer space.
Titan missiles wait underground
like restored Minotaurs
for the final sacrifice of a burning world.

We climb over heat-split stone, follow
the small scats of rabbits,
skirting turpentine bushes
that might hide a Gila Monster
or a rattler's lair.

By chance I look up to
a gargantuan Yucca tree, bathed
in the tangerine blood of last light.
Sword-haired and flat black
as a buffalo's back, it seems
to twist while its three faces muse,
unmoved by a dervish of wind.

Overshadowing us on this hill,
each of its shaggy arms ignite
into monstrous beauty.
Here is a Titan we can believe in,
rooted in the primitive landscape
of our intuition that
no computer can imagine.
Radiant with ungovernable light
this is the power that names us,
compelling as desire,
backlit by desert's blood-copper tides.
As warmth leaves the world,
                              everything is possible
and we celebrate
this giant, suddenly awake.

Green Light

Creatures that rustle in the shadows, all the crooked
deformed ones in the world, with tiny feet and far too many eyes,
can hide in the grass—that's why it's there,
silent and full of moonlight among the continents.

I have lived in the grass among the small ones who resemble
      broken twigs.
From their towers of cowslip the bumblebees came like bells
into my heart with words of a magic species.
The winds took my poem and spread it out like dust.

I have lived in the grass with the Earth and I have heard it breathe
like an animal that has walked a long way and is thirsting for the
      waterholes,
and I felt it lie down heavily on its side in the evening like a
      buffalo,
in the darkness between the stars, where there is room.

The dance of the winds and the great wildfires in the grass I
      remember often:
—The shadow play of smiles on a face that always shows
      forgiveness.
But why it has such great patience with us
deep down in its iron core, its huge magnesium heart, we are far
      from understanding.

For we have forgotten this: that the Earth is a star of grass,
a seed-planet, swirling with spores as with clouds, from sea to sea,
a whirl of them. Seeds take hold under the cobblestones
and between the letters in my poem, here they are.

> translated from the Norwegian by
> Roger Greenwald

Notes on the Contributors

AI is a native of the American Southwest. Her second book, *Killing Floor,* was the 1978 Lamont Poetry Selection of the Academy of American Poets. Her third book, *Sin,* won an American Book Award from the Before Columbus Foundation.

ANTLER lives in Milwaukee. He is the author of *Factory* and *Last Words,* and winner of the Walt Whitman Award, the Witter Bynner Prize, and a Pushcart Prize. His work appears in many anthologies.

JOHN BALABAN is the author of *Words for My Daughter,* which was selected by W.S. Merwin for the 1992 National Poetry Series. He is Director of the MFA in Creative Writing Program at the University of Miami, Coral Gables.

ELLEN BASS is the author of several volumes of poetry, including *For Earthly Survival* and *Our Stunning Harvest.* She is also co-author of *The Courage to Heal: A Guide for Women Survivors of Child Sexual Abuse.*

SUJATA BHATT was born in Ahmedabad, India, and raised in Pune, India. She now lives in Bremen, Germany. Her work has appeared in British, Irish, American, and Canadian journals. Her most recent collection of poems is *The Stinking Rose.*

PETER BLUE CLOUD (ARONIAWENRATE) is a Turtle Clan member of the Mohawk Nation at Kahnawake, Mohawk Territory (Quebec). He is the author of *Elderberry Flute Song* and *The Other Side of Nowhere.* His *Clans of Many Nations,* a collection of poetry, is forthcoming.

JOHN BRADLEY teaches at Northern Illinois University. His book, *Love-In-Idleness: The Poetry of Roberto Zingarello,* published by Word Works, won the Washington Prize.

JOHN BRANDI, wanderer, homemaker, poet, painter, lives in New Mexico and earns a living as an itinerant poet. His most recent book is *A Question of Journey.*

JOSEPH BRUCHAC is a storyteller and writer of Abenaki, English, and Slovak ancestry. His novel about the Abenaki people in pre-Columbian times, *Dawn Land,* was published in 1993.

CHRISTOPHER BUCKLEY is the editor of *What Will Sacrifice: The Ars Poetica in Contemporary Poetry* along with Christopher Merrill, for Peregrine Smith Books. His sixth book of poems is *Dark Matter.*

JERAH CHADWICK has lived on the Aleutian Island of Unalaska for the past twelve years. He has been widely published in journals and anthologies. His most recent chapbook is *From the Cradle of Storms,* published by State Street in 1990.

KELLY CHERRY is the author of fourteen books, including *God's Loud Hand* (poems), *The Exiled Heart* (autobiography), and *My Life and Dr. Joyce Brothers* (a novel in stories). She is Evjue-Bascom Professor in the Humanities at the University of Wisconsin-Madison.

ANDREA COLLINS is a poet whose work has appeared in *Agni Review, College English, Feminist Studies, Prairie Schooner, The Southern Review,* and other journals. She is the Development Director for Associated Writing Programs.

ALLAN COOPER lives in the fishing village of Alma, New Brunswick, in Canada, and is publisher of the poetry publishing house Owl's Head Press. His book *The Pearl Inside the Body: Poems Selected and New* was published in 1991.

GREGORY CORSO is one of the foremost living beat poets. He is the author of six volumes of poetry, including *Mindfield: New & Selected Poems* (1989, Thunder's Mouth Press).

WILLIAM DICKEY'S *In the Dreaming: Selected Poems* was published by the University of Arkansas Press in 1994. He died that year at the age of sixty-five

SHARON DOUBIAGO lives in her van, Psyche, west on Highway One between Tijuana, Mexico, and Victoria, Canada. Author of many books including *Psyche Drives the Coast* and *South America, Mi Hija,* she is currently working on *Son,* a book-length narrative on raising a male athlete.

EDWARD A. DOUGHERTY, a former poetry editor of the *Mid-American Review*, is a director, with his spouse, of the World Friendship Center in Hiroshima, Japan.

STEPHEN DUNN is the author of eight collections of poetry and *Walking Light: Essays and Memoirs.* W.W. Norton published his *New and Selected Poems: 1974–1994.*

W.D. EHRHART is the author of a number of books, most recently *The Distance We Travel.* He lives in Philadelphia with his wife and daughter.

NANCY EIMERS was the recipient of a 1987 *Nation* "Discovery" Award and a 1989 NEA grant. She teaches in the MFA program at Western Michigan University.

LYNN EMANUEL is the author of two books of poetry, *Hotel Fiesta* and *The Dig.* She is a recipient of two NEA Fellowships and the National Poetry Series Award and is an associate professor at the University of Pittsburgh.

JOHN ENGELS is an atomic veteran. His *Cardinals in the Ice Age* was selected by Philip Levine as one of the 1986 National Poetry Series winners. Engels' *Walking to Cootehill: New & Selected Poems, 1958–1992* was recently published.

JOHN ENGMAN has published *Alcatraz* and *Keeping Still, Mountain* and was anthologized in *New American Poets of the 90s.* He teaches writing at The Loft, the University of Minnesota, and St. Olaf College.

CAROLYN FORCHÉ's first volume of poems, *Gathering the Tribes*, won the Yale Series of Younger Poets Award. Her second volume, *The Country Between Us*, won the Lamont Poetry Selection in 1981. She edited *Against Forgetting: Twentieth Century Poetry of Witness.*

MARGARET GIBSON has published five books with Louisiana State University Press, among them *Long Walks in the Afternoon*, the Lamont Selection for 1982, and, most recently, *The Vigil*, 1993. She teaches at the University of Connecticut.

ALLEN GINSBERG is Distinguished Professor at Brooklyn College. He was selected by France's cultural ministry to receive the "Chevalier de l'Ordre des Artes et des Lettres" and has won the Harriet Monroe Poetry Award, given by the University of Chicago.

DANIELA GIOSEFFI, a poet, novelist, and essayist, has published *Women on War: Essential Voices for the Nuclear Age*, winner of the American Book Award, 1990, and *On Prejudice: A Global Perspective.* She was a founding member of The Writers & Publishers Alliance for Nuclear Disarmament, bestower of the Olive Branch Book Awards.

DIANE GLANCY teaches at Macalester College in St. Paul, Minnesota. Her collection of essays, *Claiming Breath*, won the 1993 American Book Award from the Before Columbus Foundation.

PATRICIA GOEDICKE was a resident artist spring 1993 at the Rockefeller Institute's Bellagio Study and Conference Center on Lake Como. She teaches in the Creative Writing program at the University of Montana. *Paul Bunyan's Bearskin* was her tenth book of poetry.

JAMES GRABILL lives in Portland, Oregon, and teaches at Clackamas Community College. He is the author of *One River, To Other Beings, Through the Green Fire*, and *Poem Rising Out of the Earth and Standing Up in Someone.*

JORIE GRAHAM has a new collection, *Materialism*, recently out from The Ecco Press. Previous collections include *Region of Unlikeness* and *The End of Beauty.* She lives and teaches in Iowa City.

MAXINE KUMIN's tenth collection of poems, *Looking for Luck,* was a finalist for the National Book Critics Circle Award. A collection of short stories and prose is forthcoming. Kumin lives on a farm in New Hampshire where she and her husband raise horses.

KURIHARA SADAKO was born in 1913. Like Tōge Sankichi, she was in Hiroshima when the bomb was dropped. She has published political essays as well as many volumes of poetry, including Black Eggs, which Richard Minear has translated.

BARBARA LA MORTICELLA lives in a cabin in the woods outside Portland, Oregon. She hosts a regular poetry radio show. She had a chapbook of her poems published, *Even the Hills Move in Waves,* and is working on a collection of poems.

DORIANNE LAUX is the author of *Awake,* published by BOA Editions. Her awards include an NEA grant and a Pushcart Prize. She lives in Petaluma, California.

DENISE LEVERTOV's most recent books are *Evening Train* and *New & Selected Essays.* She lives in Seattle. *Singular Voices,* edited by Stephen Berg, provides her commentary on her poem, "Gathered at the River."

LEONID LEVIN is an engineer, interpreter and translator, and a poet. Born in the Soviet Union, he emigrated to the U.S. a dozen years ago and is totally bilingual.

PHILIP LEVINE's *What Work Is* won the National Book Award. *The Bread of Time,* autobiographical writing, and *The Simple Truth,* a new book of poetry, are forthcoming. Levine, born in 1928, recently retired from Fresno State University.

ADRIAN C. LOUIS is an enrolled member of the Lovelock Paiute Indian Tribe. His most recent book of poems is *Blood Thirsty Savages,* from Time Being Books.

GEORGE MACBETH was born in Scotland and died, in 1992, in Ireland. Author of nearly twenty volumes of poetry, he is considered a major influence on British poetry.

JACK MARSHALL's most recent collection of poetry is *Sesame* (1993, Coffee House Press, Minneapolis, MN). He is a past recipient of the Pushcart Prize and the Bay Area Reviewer's Award. He lives in San Francisco.

CHARLES MARTIN teaches in the Writing Seminars at Johns Hopkins University. Among his books of poetry are *Steal the Bacon* and *Catullus.*

THOMAS MCGRATH served in the Army Air Forces in World War II. He was blacklisted in 1954 for refusing to cooperate with the House Committee on Un-American Activities. He died in 1990.

DAVID McKAIN is the author of three books of poetry. His book *Spellbound: Growing Up in God's Country* won the Associated Writing Program Award for Creative Non-fiction.

GARY METRAS holds degrees from U. Mass-Amherst and Goddard College. His poems have appeared in *Another Chicago Magazine, Crosscurrents, Connecticut Poetry Review, Poetry East,* and *Yarrow.* His most recent chapbook is *Seven Stones for Seven Poems.*

RICHARD H. MINEAR is professor of History at the University of Massachusetts, Amherst, and translator of *Requiem for Battleship Yamato, Hiroshima: Three Witnesses,* and *Black Eggs,* poems by Kurihara Sadako.

HONOR MOORE's collection of poems, *Memoir,* was published in 1988. She was the 1992 winner of an artist's grant from the Connecticut Commission on the Arts, and is completing a biography of her grandmother, the painter Margaret Sargent, which will be published by Viking in 1995.

ROBERT MORGAN, a native of North Carolina, has taught at Cornell since 1971. His most recent books of poems are *Sigodlin* and *Green River: New and Selected Poems. Good Measure: Essays, Interviews and Notes on Poetry* was published in 1993.

DAVID MURA is the author of *After We Lost Our Way,* which was a 1989 National Poetry Series winner and will be reprinted by Story Line Press, and *Turning Japanese: Memoirs of a Sansei* (Doubleday), which won a PEN Josephine Miles Book Award.

ALAN NAPIER is a poet and computer artist. His poems have appeared in *The American Poetry Review, Chelsea, The Southern Poetry Review,* and many other journals. He manages a screen printing company.

LORINE NIEDECKER was born and died in Fort Atkinson, Wisconsin. Cid Corman says of her: "Wisconsin's finest quietest most resonant poet: (1903–1970) — a quarter of a century after her death finally becoming known."

NAOMI SHIHAB NYE edited *This Same Sky,* a collection of poems from around the world, and has a children's picture book, *Sitti's Secrets,* about her Palestinian grandmother, forthcoming. She lives in San Antonio.

SHARON OLDS teaches at New York University and at Goldwater Hospital (for the severely disabled). She has published four volumes of poetry, the most recent of which is *The Father.*

PETER ORESICK is Assistant Director of the University of Pittsburgh Press. His books include *Definitions, Working Classics: Poems on Industrial Life,* and *The Pittsburgh Book of Contemporary American Poetry.*

ALICIA OSTRIKER is the author of seven volumes of poetry, most recently *Green Age*, published by the University of Pittsburgh Press. Her most recent book of criticism is *Feminist Revision and the Bible* (Blackwell).

ANTONIA QUINTANA PIGNO is a native New Mexican and teaches Spanish at Kansas State University. Her work has appeared in national and international literary magazines. Three fine press, limited editions of her poetry have been published by the Zauberberg Press, Coffeyville, Kansas.

DAVID RAY is a professor of English at the University of Missouri-Kansas City. His most recent books are *Not Far from the River* and *The Maharani's New Wall*, which was nominated for a Pulitzer Prize. He has been a recipient of a NEA award for his fiction.

JUDY RAY is the Executive Director of The Writer's Place in Kansas City. Her most recent books are *The Jaipur Sketchbook: Impressions of India* and *Pigeons in the Chandeliers*.

ADRIENNE RICH's most recent book of poems is *An Atlas of the Difficult World*. *What Is Found There: Notebooks on Poetry and Politics* was published in 1993.

ELISAVIETTA RITCHIE's *Flying Time: Stories & Half-Stories* includes four PEN Syndicated Fiction winners. *The Arc of the Storm* and *A Wound-Up Cat and Other Bedtime Stories* are her newest poetry collections.

DAVID ROMTVEDT lives in Buffalo, Wyoming. His book of poetry *A Flower Whose Name I Do Not Know* was a 1991 National Poetry Series selection.

BENJAMIN ALIRE SÁENZ won an American Book Award in 1991 for his first book of poetry, *Calendar of Dust*. He is also the author of a collection of short stories, *Flowers for the Broken*, and a second book of poetry, *Dark and Perfect Angels*. He teaches Creative Writing at the University of Texas at El Paso.

NANAO SAKAKI was drafted into the Japanese navy in WWII where he served as a radar analyst. He identified the B-29 on its way to bomb Nagasaki on his radar screen. He is the author of *Break the Mirror*, North Point Press, 1987.

MARY JO SALTER is the author of two volumes of poems, *Henry Purcell in Japan* and *Unfinished Painting*. She teaches at Mount Holyoke College.

NICHOLAS SAMARAS won the 1991 Yale Series of Younger Poets Award for his book *Hands of the Saddlemaker*. He is presently working on his second and third poetry collections.

MARK SANDERS grew up in Nebraska, 150 miles west of the SAC base, and lived in northwest Missouri, near many missile silos. He currently lives in League City, Texas, where he teaches at College of the Mainland.

DANIEL SIMKO was born in Czechoslovakia and came to this country shortly after the events of 1968. He is the author of a book of translations by Georg Trakl, *Autumn Sonata,* which won the Poets House Translation Award in 1988.

MAURYA SIMON was born in 1950 in New York City. She has published three volumes of poetry: *The Enchanted Room, Days of Awe,* and *Speaking in Tongues.* She currently teaches in the Creative Writing Department at the University of California, Riverside, and lives on Mt. Baldy in Southern California.

LYUBOV SIROTA and her son, both exposed to the Chernobyl fallout in the city of Pripyat, have spent much time in the hospital for treatment of radiation sickness. Sirota's poems have appeared in the U.S, Canada, and Western Europe.

GARY SNYDER has published fifteen books of poetry and prose. His book *Turtle Island* won the Pulitzer Prize for poetry in 1975. Since 1985 he has been a member of the faculty at UC Davis, 108 miles downstream from his mountain place.

ELIZABETH SPIRES is the author of three books of poems: *Globe, Swan's Island,* and *Annonciade.* She lives in Baltimore and teaches at Goucher College and in the Writing Seminars at Johns Hopkins University.

WILLIAM STAFFORD, author of many books of poetry, has acted as Poetry Consultant for The Library of Congress. His account of serving as a conscientious objector in World War II, *Down in My Heart,* was published by The Bench Press. He died in 1993.

MARK STRAND was born in Canada, but has lived his entire adult life in the U.S. He currently lives in Salt Lake City, Utah. His most recent books are *The Continuous Life* and *Dark Harbor.*

STEPHANIE STRICKLAND's *The Red Virgin: A Poem of Simone Weil* won the 1993 Brittingham Prize from the University of Wisconsin Press. Her collection *Give the Body Back* is from the University of Missouri.

LUCIEN STRYK's *Collected Poems* appeared in 1984. In 1993, he published *Zen Poems of China and Japan: The Crane's Bill* and in 1994, *Zen Poetry: Let the Spring Breeze Enter. Zen, Poetry, The Art of Lucien Stryk,* edited by Susan Porterfield, a collection of works by and about Stryk, appeared in 1993.

AMBER COVERDALE SUMRALL lives in Santa Cruz, California, and is co-editor of *Catholic Girls & Boys, The Time of Our Lives: Women Write on Sex after 40,* and *Women of the 14th Moon: Writings on Menopause.* She is editor of *Breaking Up Is Hard to Do* and *Love's Shadow: Stories by Women.*

SHINKICHI TAKAHASHI (1901–87) is thought by the Japanese to be their greatest modern Zen poet. His Zen poems, translated by Lucien Stryk and Takashi Ikemoto, are available in *Triumph of the Sparrow.*

JAMES TATE's *Selected Poems* received the Pulitzer Prize and the William Carlos Williams Award. His most recent book is *Worshipful Company of Fletchers.*

TŌGE SANKICHI (1917–53) has been called "a lyric poet from cradle to grave." He was an activist and a member of the Communist Party after 1949. He is the author of *Poems of the Atomic Bomb*, which Richard Minear translated in *Hiroshima: Three Witnesses.*

EDWINA TRENTHAM was born and grew up in Bermuda. She was a fellow at Yaddo in 1989. She currently teaches English at Asnuntuck Community College in Enfield, Connecticut.

PAMELA USCHUK lives in southwest Colorado. She has taught fiction and poetry through Marist College at Green Haven Maximum Security Prison in New York. She won the 1989 *Ascent* Poetry Prize from the University of Illinois.

ROBERT VASQUEZ was a Stegner Fellow at Stanford University and Kings-Park-Chavez Visiting Professor of English at Western Michigan University. He teaches at College of the Sequoias in Visalia, California. His poetry appears in *After Aztlan: Latino Poets of the Nineties.*

RONALD WALLACE is Director of Creative Writing at the University of Wisconsin in Madison. His twelve books and chapbooks include *People and Dog in the Sun* and *The Makings of Happiness,* both published by the University of Pittsburgh Press. He divides his time between Madison and a forty-acre farm in Bear Valley, Wisconsin.

RICHARD WILBUR, who was the nation's second Poet Laureate, received his second Pulitzer Prize for his *New and Collected Poems* (1988). He and his wife live in Key West, Florida, and Cummington, Massachusetts.

BERYLE WILLIAMS lives in Estes Park, Colorado. Her poems and essays have appeared in numerous journals and in anthologies from Milkweed Editions, New Rivers Press, and Papier-Mache Press. She has taught English and creative writing at Beijing University in China.

C.K. WILLIAMS' most recent book is *A Dream of Mind.* His *Selected Poems* was published in 1994 and a book of selected prose will be published in 1995.

ELEANOR WILNER is the author of four books of poems: *Otherwise, Sarah's Choice, Shekinah,* and *maya.* Currently a MacArthur Fellow, she teaches in the MFA Program for Writers, Warren Wilson College.

S.L. WISENBERG usually lives in Chicago and often writes about memory and history. Her work has appeared in *The New Yorker, The Kenyon Review, The North American Review,* and many anthologies.

WILLIAM WITHERUP has published two books of poetry on nuclear themes. He is presently at work on *Dancing with the Radon Daughters* (poetry), and *Ma Witherup's Top Secret Cherry Pie* (essay-memoirs).

C.D. WRIGHT received a writer's fellowship from the Lila Wallace Foundation. Her booklength poem *Just Whistle* was published by Kelsey Street Press in Berkeley.

PAUL ZIMMER is the director of the University of Iowa Press. He lives in Iowa City with his wife, Suzanne, and, whenever possible, at their farm in southwest Wisconsin. His most recent book of poetry is *Big Blue Train*.

Acknowledgements

AI. "The Testimony of J. Robert Oppenheimer" is reprinted from *Sin* by Ai. Copyright © 1986 by Ai. Reprinted by permission of Houghton Mifflin Company. All rights reserved.

ANTLER. "Bringing Zeus to His Knees" appeared in *Last Words* (Ballantine) by Antler. Reprinted with author's permission.

JOHN BALABAN. "Atomic Ghost" from *Words for My Daughter.* Copyright © 1991 by John Balaban. Used by permission of the author and Copper Canyon Press, P.O. Box 271, Port Townsend, WA 98368.

ELLEN BASS. "They're Family Men" is reprinted from *Our Stunning Harvest* (New Society Press) by permission of the author. Copyright © 1985 by Ellen Bass.

SUJATA BHATT. "Wine from Bordeaux" is reprinted from *Monkey Shadows.* Copyright © 1991 by Sujata Bhatt. Used by permission of the author and Carcanet Press Limited, 208-212 Corn Exchange, Manchester M4 3BQ, England.

PETER BLUE CLOUD (ARONIAWENRATE). "Deeper than a Dream" is used by permission of the author and Empty Bowl.

JOHN BRADLEY. "Sailors Shielding Their Eyes During Atomic Bomb Test, Bikini, 1947" first published in the *Cincinnati Poetry Review.* Used by permission of the author.

JOHN BRANDI. "Preparing the Nets" appeared in *Hymn for a Night Feast* (Holy Cow!). Used by permission of the author.

JOSEPH BRUCHAC. "Wahsah Zeh (War Dance)—As Long as the Grass" appeared, in an earlier version, in *Nuke Chronicles* (Contact II Publications). Copyright © 1985 by Joseph Bruchac. Used by permission of the author.

CHRISTOPHER BUCKLEY. "Why I'm in Favor of a Nuclear Freeze," from *Dust Light, Leaves,* published by Vanderbilt University Press. Copyright © 1986 by Christopher Buckley. Used with permission of the author.

JERAH CHADWICK. "Eight-legged Colt, Chernobyl" is used by permission of the author.

KELLY CHERRY. "Prayer for a Future Beyond Ideology and War" by Kelly Cherry, in *Natural Theology,* copyright © 1988 by Kelly Cherry. Used by permission of Louisiana State University Press.

Index

COLOPHON

This book was set in Spectrum and Albertus typefaces, with Reactor face for the title on the front cover. Coffee House Press books are printed on acid free paper and are smyth sewn for durability and reading comfort.